Room 217

The Making of a Teacher

Room 217
The Making of a Teacher

ISBN 13: 978-1-73233-362-8
ISBN 10: 1-73233-362-9
Library of Congress PCN 2019934408

Inquiries should be addressed to
www.amitypublications.com

To contact the author, please visit
www.stephen-mackenzie.com

This book is dedicated to all the students I have encountered in and around my classroom over the last twenty-plus years: you have blessed my life in unimaginable ways.

It is also dedicated Rod Doherty and Mary Pat Rowland who gave me my first start as a writer, publishing my column, Room 217, in Foster's Daily Democrat, Dover, NH for nearly nine years, and especially to my faithful readers of that column. I cannot thank you enough for your emails, cards, and notes of affirmation and support.

Author's Note

From late summer 2006 through mid-2015 I wrote a column for Foster's Daily Democrat, the daily newspaper for Dover, NH and the surrounding seacoast area of New Hampshire and southern Maine. It was called Room 217, the room at Somersworth High School, Somersworth, NH, that for most of the last twenty-plus years has been a second home for me. Contained in these pages is what I hope will be volume one of those columns.

Now even as an English teacher, I cannot guarantee that this book is 100% free of errors or typos. Like the math teacher who made a rare error in calculation or the history teacher who got a date slightly wrong, I am only human. I can guarantee, however, you won't find anything like some of the commentary spoken by one of our Boston sports announcers, like, "He probably could've went for third," or "Man, Pedroia would've 'ate-en' that up."

It has been fun for me to go back through these old columns in preparing the manuscript for this book, reliving old experiences and recalling old friends. I hope you enjoy reading about them—or in some cases rereading. I love hearing from readers, so if you are inclined share some of your thoughts or reactions with me please feel free to email me at stephen@stephen-mackenzie.com. I always respond to emails and look forward to receiving them. You may also visit my website at www.stephen-mackenzie.com.

Table of Contents

INTRODUCTION

I often get asked why, at nearly forty-years-old, I decided to become a teacher. See, I had never gone to college, so I had to earn both Bachelor's and Master's degrees, taking up four years of my life and about 30k in student loan debt, all for a job that paid less money than I had made since I was nineteen years old. Sometimes it comes from friends, sometimes from colleagues, sometimes from students. It's not an unreasonable question, and it's not one I have any difficulty answering.

It was during the fall of 1990 that some friends from church approached me about managing our church's summer camp, Wanakee, in Meredith, NH. The personnel committee and other church leaders were changing the manager's job description, combining the summer responsibilities with year-round youth work, and creating a new position called Director of Youth Ministries. The problem was they would not be ready to fill this new position until early 1992, which left them needing a one-year interim manager for Wanakee for the 1991 summer season. Because I had both the time and the managerial experience they were looking for, I agreed to help them out.

I would not be stretching the truth to say, we had an incredible season. We were able to hire an outstanding staff from the kitchen to the waterfront, grounds crew, and counselors. Each one wanted to make a difference in the lives of the campers. We all met together for the first time on day one of training week. Six days later we were truly a family. Shortly after that, camp opened, and the first adult volunteers and one hundred plus kids arrived and we were off.

It seemed that we got stronger with each successive week of the season. The permanent staff felt good about what they were doing. The weekly volunteers regularly gave strong, positive feedback at our end-of-camp wrap-up meetings. The individual event directors were highly complimentary of both me and the staff. Our spirits were high and the Spirit was obviously present.

As the personnel committee began to finalize its plans and the job description, event directors, parents, staff members, volunteer counselors, even some of the older campers began to encourage me to apply for the new year-round position. I responded cordially to their praises and politely declined saying, "I agreed to a one-year job as interim. I don't think I want to work full-time for the church, my part-time music director job is sufficient, I don't want to move, and I really don't want to work for a committee."

But the pleas continued. "Steve, have you considered applying for the year-round job?" "Steve, you are going to apply for the new position, aren't you?" "Steve, things are so awesome here this year—you really should apply for the new position." "Steve, you have to apply for the new position." Even members of the search committee, many of whom were my friends, began encouraging me to apply. Several of them all but told me that after this incredible season the odds of my not getting the job were almost nil.

Okay, I will confess that I did, once or twice, give the idea a fleeting thought, but my position moved only from impossible to improbable. It wasn't until one of my closest friends, also one of my former pastors, bumped into me during his week as an event director, wrapped me up in this big bear hug and said, "Stephen, you have found your niche; you have to apply for this job," that I actually began to think about the possibility.

Eventually, my wife and I began talking about what life might look like if in fact I decided to apply for the job. We considered what we'd do with our house, what she might look for in terms of a job, and what living in the farmhouse at Wanakee would be like. More importantly we took a close look at the summer and how well it had gone, how natural the manager's job felt for me, and how much she enjoyed heading up the kitchen. It really had been an incredible experience—one that just felt right, more of a calling than a job, something I was supposed to do. It began to dawn on me that maybe it *was* something I was supposed to continue doing.

After much consideration, soul searching, yes, even praying I eventually caved and decided to go for it. We began to actually consider, from all of my informal conversations, the probability that I would be hired. We started to formulate ideas, make plans, get excited. It wasn't long before I moved from considering the job to wanting the job, to wanting it more than I had ever wanted any job in my life. Add to that the fact that the job was mine, essentially for the applying, and I was beside myself with excitement and anticipation.

Sometime after the search and interview process was completed, we invited some friends over for dinner, one of whom was the chair of the search committee. He asked if we could chat about the job before he left and I eagerly awaited everyone else's departure after dinner. As the last person left I remember thinking, *Ah, the moment I've been waiting for.* "Well, Steve, we made our decision . . . and it wasn't you."

I usually stop there, at least for a few seconds. The first several times I told the story I *had* to stop there, to collect myself. My students are typically very responsive in a positive way, especially after I confirm for them how absolutely devastated I was, and that two months later the devastation was trebled when

3

my father unexpectedly dropped dead of a massive heart attack.

Yet I never end the story there. I always add, *Yes, not getting that job was shattering. Even now, years later, there is no doubt in my mind that had I gotten it I would have loved it and I would have been good at it . . . but if I had gotten that job I would never have become a teacher, and I can't even begin to fathom that.* You see, the most important thing about that summer was discovering, at thirty-five years old, just how incredible it was to work full-time with kids, that making a difference in the life of a kid is just about as good as it gets. So once I realized that a bruised, even battered, ego is not fatal, that my self-worth is determined by me not a search committee, I nursed my self-esteem back to healthy, and enrolled as a full-time student at UNH. Three years later, including sixteen-credit summers, I graduated with my BA in English. Twelve months after that I had completed my MA in English Lit., and in the fall of 1997, at Somersworth High School, Somersworth, NH, I began the most incredible career of my life. It has not stopped yet.

It was only two years ago. I was teaching a freshmen English class and sometime in December I mentioned that soon after the end of the semester in late January I would be leaving. Matt, a student who especially enjoyed my class, queried, "What do you mean you'll be leaving." I explained that since I had "fake retired" three years earlier I only teach in the first semester, then I leave for the rest of the winter. He looked at me and said, "Wow! You mean we just got lucky?" I looked right back and replied, "No, dude, *I'm* the one who got lucky!"

When they first meet me, my kids don't quite understand why I think I have the best job in the world. I had this one kid, Josh, several years ago, who walked in and flopped into his seat one Monday. I looked up from my desk and said, "Goooood morning, Josh! How was your weekend?" He slowly turned toward me and responded, reluctantly, "Mr. MacKenzie, you are way too happy for a Monday morning." I smiled, thought for a moment, and then said, "Josh, I want you to think about Wednesday evenings, when you are at youth group doing the things you love most with people you love best." He stared at me intently for a few seconds and then replied, "That's how it is for you on Monday mornings?" "That's how it is for me on Monday mornings." Most of them eventually get it—why I love my job so much. By the time you're done reading this book, I hope you will, too. When you get right down to it, I probably should write that search committee a "thank you" note.

PART I

EXPECTATIONS

The first assignment I give at the beginning of a course is frequently this: I want you to write me a one-page personal letter in which you must, no matter what else you say, address two things: I want to know what your expectations are for this course and I want to learn something about you. So let me share a snippet about what my expectations were when I went into teaching, and perhaps reveal something about me.

I matriculated to the University of New Hampshire in January of 1994 after having done some summer and fall work at what was then UNH's College for Life-long Learning, or CLL. Once on the UNH Durham campus I was what one refers to as a non-traditional student, or a Non-trad. In other words, compared to the traditional eighteen or nineteen-year-old traditional college freshman, I was, by kid standards, old—thirty-six to be exact. By the time I started teaching full-time at Somersworth High School I was almost two months past my fortieth birthday. So my expectations were considerably different, I suspect, than they might otherwise have been nearly twenty years earlier.

Of course, even at forty, I was technically just entering my "prime" working years. I had little teaching experience, but had worked with kids in one capacity or another for most of my adult life. So I did not come to the classroom naïve. I knew kids liked to push boundaries. Many of them drank and smoked a lot of pot. Some even dabbled in stronger drugs. Others lived in homes where there was too little supervision, or not enough money, or abuse and neglect, or all of the above.

Then there were many of my students who came from great homes with caring and involved parents, who had every socio-economic advantage. I had both affluent students and students who lived below the poverty level, who worked hard to achieve, did their homework, and participated regularly in our classroom experiences. I had students whose goal in life was to graduate high school prepared for college, or the military, or the workplace. Going into my first semester, I expected to win them all—every single one of them. I did not.

I quickly learned I would never win everyone, nobody can do that. My expectation changed a bit. I decided what I really wanted was not to make their lives any more difficult than they already might be; I didn't want school, at least my classroom, to be one more aggravation to them. I might not be able to "win" them, but I could still love them and show them the respect they deserve.

Through that first assignment, I have had many expectations shared (some theirs and some mine), and I've learned much about my students over the years. I learned some hated English. Many hated reading, especially aloud in class, and even more hated writing. I've learned some loved reading and writing and couldn't wait to get started. I learned some didn't want to be judged by their past, or by the past of an older sibling. And some held the deluded expectation that there wouldn't be too much homework. Most of them, though, in some way or another, voiced the fact that they wanted, even expected, the class to be fun. I hope it was.

Back in School

"Hey Mr. Mack," somebody whined, "why do you assign this stuff? I can't write five or six paragraphs about something that got me to this point in my life. Even if I could it'd be stupid and nobody would want to read it."

"Of course you can," I responded, "and I guarantee at least one other person will want to read it—me! I'll tell you what, I'll do the assignment along with you."

I'm not sure if my shivers were from the biting cold or from fear as I made my way up the granite steps of Hamilton Smith Hall one January afternoon in 1994. At thirty-six, this was my first class as a student in nearly two decades; Freshman English no less. As if being a non-traditional student wasn't bad enough, I was having to repeat a class I'd begun some eighteen years earlier, in order to erase an Administrative Failure I'd received. See, I didn't know enough back then to withdraw from the course, so I just quit going when it demanded more than I wanted to give, which at that point in my life wasn't too much. I'd only taken two courses, but they were both there to greet me upon my return to UNH, including the "AF," even after all those years. Not only did I not want to take the course again, but I'd have to take it with a bunch of teeny-boppin', freshmen party animals, most of whom probably majored in fraternity.

I have to admit I was feeling a little bit scared. I found the room and slipped into a desk near the door, willing myself to blend in. There were at least twenty students in the class. I looked around taking in Coed Naked T-shirts, baseball hats—frontwards and backwards—Champion sweatshirts, CK and Guess jeans.

There were buzz cuts, bowl cuts and never cuts. They had L.L. Bean backpacks, EMS and Eastpak brand backpacks. Some students were casually chatting with their neighbors. Some were sitting up straight, staring into emptiness. Some were slouched, legs stuck out, spread slightly, one foot twisted to the side, the other pointing up, as if they had taken great pains to strike the most careless looking position possible.

Oh great! Here I am. My jeans are Levis, my T-shirt is a no name and my backpack came from Ames. I'm almost old enough to be their father. Green Day is a rock group? I though it was a . . . no, that's Green Peace. I don't think I should be here. When *I* was in retail CK stood for Chess King. *Bad* is good. *Cool* is back. I'm getting crow's feet and gray hair. Some of these guys don't even shave yet. Why am I doing this? I left a good job worth about fifty grand a year. I could go back to work for them tomorrow. Surely I can't want to teach that bad! I guess I did, though, because I kept going. Of course, I do have to admit I broke down and bought a pair of Timberland boots—I convinced myself it was to keep my feet warm truckin' across campus in the winter.

I convinced myself of a lot during those early years, like the importance of taking my classes seriously. Yup, I actually took Freud and all of his phallic symbol, male-envy stuff seriously, so I could get through Human Development 401. And, I'll never forget the first words out of my professor's mouth when I began The Romantic Period: "Well, I'm assuming you're all here because you love poetry." *What? I freakin' hate poetry!* But I learned about Wordsworth's "Winding Brook" and Coleridge's "Kubla Kahn," whatever it is, because I needed the class. I even convinced myself to seriously study about those obscure Yanomamo people somewhere down in South America, and the Sinhalese and Tamils of Sri Lanka, because Anthropology 411 fulfilled a required history Gen. Ed. And you know, given a few more weeks, my Food and

People course might actually have convinced me that I *do* drink too much coffee—but probably not. All this because somewhere in me I realized that I *did* want to teach *that* bad.

It wasn't long before I strolled up the walk to Ham Smith as if I were headed home, trademark coffee mug in hand and book bag slung over one shoulder, stopping for a junk food fix from the vending machine on my way to class. I learned to look forward to the start of each semester, to enjoy the challenges each course offered, the new books, problems, students, instructors. I learned Shakespeare can be really fun, a little perverted at times but fun. Most importantly, I learned I don't have to love everything, like it's okay if Grendle and his mother don't interest me in the least and I hated Huxley's *Brave New World*—I don't have to like it all, I just have to do it!

Take my student loans, for example. I don't have to like them; I just have to have them—because I *have* to! So what if I end up paying on them for the rest of my working life? I keep remembering what Christa McCaullife said about teaching: "I touch the future; I teach." See, the way I look at it is this, millions of people pay on a mortgage for most of their lives and when they're done they own a house. I may pay on my student loans the rest of my life, but I'll touch the future. Oh, by the way, I was wrong about those freshmen in English 401; we had a blast. That course, students, instructor and content; silly, annoying, administratively failed Freshman English, is why I declared English as my major.

Now, F7, spell-check's done, Format menu, Paragraph, Line Spacing, arrow down to "double," click, and Print. "Okay, you guys, you done?"

This column, slightly revised, originally appeared in Foster's Daily Democrat on September 14, 2006.

Day One

My name is on the white board, a laminated "Color My World" poster is up on the bulletin board, the tables and chairs are in a perfect "U," textbooks are stacked neatly on the extra table. Beside them I have lined up registration cards, emergency cards, Internet Use Agreements, and Free or Reduced Lunch forms. I have family pictures on my desk, a boom box on a side table, and two philodendrons hanging in the windows. I write my first saying-of-the-day on the board, taken from one of my mother's old desk calendars: *If you're always dwelling on trouble, change your address.* I'm ready. Bring on the kids. And come they did. Twenty-nine in all—okay, twenty-seven, two cut. Anyway, it was a heck of a lot of kids for one new teacher.

Now you should know my only other teaching job was as a music teacher at Saint Mary Academy, where when I walked into a classroom and said "good morning boys and girls" the students immediately stood beside their desks and said, in unison, "Good morning Mr. MacKenzie, God bless you." Today, my "good morning ladies and gentlemen" was met with a bunch of blank, bored, yeah-whatever stares.

Determined to teach "outside the box," university-babble for newer is better, I decided to try the *human* approach—the be-real-with-them-and-they'll-respond approach—and tell them a little bit about myself. I started off by saying my name is Mr. MacKenzie, I was born in Dover, grew up in Rollinsford, and now live here in Somersworth. I graduated from Dover High in 1975 but didn't start college until 1994, which was actually a lie since I did take two courses back in '76 but since I didn't finish one and did poorly in the other I don't count them. I told them I'd gotten married in 1978, worked in the private sector for fifteen years, and ran my own small business as a residential builder—and I really love teaching! It didn't work.

When I was done I asked if anyone had any questions before we moved on. This one girl raised her hand and asked, "Are you a real teacher?" Certain I'd not heard her correctly I responded, "Excuse me?" She repeated, a bit more sarcastically, "Are you a *real* teacher?" How does one respond to that? I thought for a minute and replied, "As opposed to what, a fake teacher?" Not about to be put off she fired back," Well, last year they hired this guy to teach chemistry who wasn't even a teacher, 'cause they couldn't find anybody else." Feeling a bit flushed I thought, *this is not why I became a teacher.*

Block two was little different, except even bigger. In fact, it was so big we couldn't even meet in my classroom; we held classes in the lecture hall. I found myself staring not at twenty-seven students, or even twenty-nine, but thirty-six students! It wasn't a class it was a convention. This time when I got done with my *human approach* spiel, one kid said to me, "You know, no offense or anything, but I only signed up for this class 'cause I wanted to have Ms. Jackman—she was the best teacher we had in this school." I straightened my bruised ego, tightened my composure, and responded with the steadiest voice I could find that I would try my hardest to be the very best Mr. MacKenzie I could be but that I could not be Ms. Jackman. *This is not why I became a teacher.*

My block three prep flew by and then it was block four. Ninety minutes more and I'm done for the day. It can't be worse than the other two. I can do this! Oh my gosh was I wrong. This class made the other two look like one of my third grade music classes at SMA, singing "The Wishy-Washy Washer Woman," You're a

13

Grand Old Flag," and "Jesus Loves Me." It took me twenty minutes to get through attendance, another twenty to get through all the complaining about why we had to read books and write papers, and another fifteen to stop one fight and fend off another. By the time we actually got working on E.B.White's "Once More to the Lake," the *first* thing on my lesson plans, I was ready to jump in it! And by the time the bell rang I was ready to drown in it! *This is definitely not why I became a teacher.*

I scanned the room. The tables were in a broken "Z," only half the chairs were put up, there were papers all over the floor, drink containers on the tables, and someone had stuck pushpins through all of the people's eyes on my brand new, twenty-five dollar laminated poster. I had been accused of being a joke, a bore, and a fraud. I glanced at the upper left-hand corner of the white board, then the clock, and realized mother was right, it was definitely time to change my address. I had to go home. So I quickly pulled my stuff together and headed out. I was almost to the front door when one of my block four students saw me. I couldn't avoid him so I nodded and tried to keep moving. But I slowed down when he smiled. He said, "Hey, Mr. Mac! You know I really liked that essay we read, that one about going to the lake. It reminded me of a camping trip I took last summer. That's what I'm going to write my reader response about. I hope you'll like it." I assure him I will, and as he started to move away he said, "Well, see ya tomorrow." Watching him go I stood there thinking, now *this* is why I became a teacher. Today, "Hey, Mr. Mack, I really liked that essay." Tomorrow, who knows, maybe "Good morning Mr. MacKenzie, God bless you!"

This column originally appeared in Foster's Daily Democrat, Dover, NH on August 31, 2006.

Heaven's Here

The new school year has begun. I've spent hours getting my room set up. The boxes have been unpacked, tables and chairs have been arranged and washed, the plants have moved back in, my computer has been put back together, my desk has been cleaned out and organized, and my "We Are Family" sign has been tacked up. I have also spent several hours in faculty and department meetings, getting syllabi ready, rosters set up in the computer, forms laid out, and books counted. Finally the kids came.

I have sixty-five students this semester in three classes, two sections of Honors English IV and one section of English I. One of the challenges I enjoy is learning all the new names. I have a girl named Dani and a boy named Danny. I have an Osbon and an Osborne, a Tyler and a Taylor, a Samantha and a Samantha-jo, a Robert who goes by Bobby (but who looks just like his older brother John who I had several years ago), and a Jennifer who goes by Juma. I have a Gabby, a Maxfield, and a Bennington. I have precious names like Crystal and Ambar, and biblical names like Caleb, Jacob, Elizabeth, and Andrew. I even have a Heaven. But what to do with them? As always, I have busy days ahead.

We're off to a fast start, though. I already have their first five assignments in, graded, and passed back. Assignment number one for all three classes was to write me a one-page personal letter in which I wanted to hear about their expectations for the course and learn something about them. From that point I have assigned several readings, including Tolstoy's "How Much Land Does a Man Need," Graffin's "Anarchy in the Tenth Grade," Stockton's, "The Lady, or the Tiger?" Thurber's "The Secret Life of Walter Mitty," and several selections from the Bible, including the story of Noah, the parable of The Prodigal Son, and the story of Ruth and Naomi, via our World Lit text. The seniors have also begun their first of four major papers, a five to seven page personal narrative: Times New Roman, twelve point font, double spaced, one inch margins all around, MLA formatting, including proper heading and pagination. Oh, and my seniors have watched Joseph and the Amazing Technicolor Dream Coat while the freshmen took in The Ron Clark Story.

So what have we turned up so far? Well, we've learned from Tolstoy that all the land we really *need* is a six by six plot. We've learned from Greg Graffin that growing up "punk" has, like most things in life, its advantages—and its disadvantages. We've learned that Walter and Mrs. Mitty need some lessons in communication and that there is little difference between semi-barbaric and completely barbaric (you really should read "The Lady, or the Tiger"). And we've shared some strong opinions on how well Andrew Lloyd Webber depicted the story of Joseph and his Coat of Many Colors. One student wrote that "hidden under the bright colors and the dancing and singing, I learned something from Joseph: It is okay to forgive people," while another wrote that "the whole movie to me was Pink Floyd and Willy Wonka mixed with a Bible story." Chocolate and vanilla my foot; in my classes we go from double fudge nut brownie to peppermint stick caramel swirl with jimmies!

Fortunately, I've discovered that most of my students really want to be successful in my class. Nearly all value education and want to graduate from high school. The majority want to go on to college. And their first assignment letters really put the pressure on. One wrote that he enjoyed independent learning "much more then (sic) any teacher would expect." He also said, "I believe that my expectations can only go as far as my determination."

Another said, "I hope everything I learn in this class I can keep using in life, looking back and saying, 'Hey, I remember when Mr. Mac taught me that.'" Another writes that she expects to come out of my class having "tremendously expanded [her] vocabulary [and] feel more at ease [with] lengthy papers and class discussions in preparation for college." Another took a bit more risk writing, "I also hear that you're quite the Republican, which made me a tad iffy at first." And yet another wrote that "ever since I met you my sophomore year in the hall, I knew . . . I would take your class my senior year."

Clearly, my semester is already in hyper-drive. I've got a bunch of new names to memorize. I've got to help some figure out whether a black Mohawk with fishnet stockings is an advantage or disadvantage (for them!). I've got to expand vocabularies (and I can't do it by puking up chocolate milk like Ron Clark!), help ease the pain of long papers, stop calling Bobby, John, help them figure out the difference between *then* and *than*, and demonstrate that Republicans can teach. I've got to convince some that Andrew Lloyd Webber was not a druggie, and my hall buddy that his three-year wait was worth it.

How am I going to do all that? Well, like the sign says: We Are Family. And like most families who have to pack too much stuff into too little a space, we have to get creative. Tomorrow I'm going to be balancing on high beams and swinging from the trees on a ropes course with my seniors as we work to build a learning machine (and maybe discover a few new flavors of ice cream). Then I'm going to help a bunch of freshmen compete for Cheez-Its and chocolate chip cookies while we learn about *plot, character, point-of-view, setting,* and *theme*. And during all that, across the room will be Heaven. What are you doing tomorrow?

This column originally appeared in Foster's Daily Democrat, Dover, NH on September 13, 2007.

Doing Better

I think teachers, me included, too often decide that if a student isn't doing well it is because they don't want to do well, at least they don't want to badly enough. We frequently find ourselves saying things like, *why don't you try harder? Why don't you study more? Why don't you come in for extra help? Don't you want to do better?* We don't always consider the fact that there may well be other forces at work which influence the answers to those questions—things beyond simple will or desire.

Lucy (not her real name) was in my class a few years ago and I have never forgotten her. She probably had as much influence on my teaching as any other student I've ever had. She was a very weak reader. She struggled with composition—even more with spelling. Asking Lucy to write a standard five paragraph essay was like asking some students to write an eight to ten-page research paper. The fact was Lucy had a learning disability in the area of language skills. It wasn't that she didn't want to do better. It was that, at best it was incredibly difficult for her, at worst it was nearly impossible.

As I began to get to know Lucy I could see how the learning disability might have solidified its grip on her life. I think there were two other siblings in the house, a working mother (with a new boyfriend on the side), and a father who had moved out of the house after many years of living together. There was clearly very little home support for anything much beyond paying the bills. By the time she was in high school, already several years behind her peer group, Lucy spent as many days at home in her room smoking cigarettes and pot as she did going to school. I mean what the heck, go to school and struggle with the work, or stay home and get high . . . hum.

Still, I had a soft spot for Lucy. I knew she liked and respected me, and I her. I also knew that she put a lot of effort into my class—at least more than was her habit in most classes. She stated coming to school more often. She would read aloud in class, knowing I did not tolerate anyone making fun of anyone else. She wrote papers, even though they were a tremendous struggle. Little by little Lucy was making some progress.

We began our poetry unit on a Monday morning with Langston Hughes' "Dream Deferred." The essence of Hughes's purpose in this short verse, a long question actually, is to challenge the way we look at and deal with the reality of not always getting what we want when we want it. We read and analyzed the work in class. We asked ourselves and each other if we simply sugarcoat our problems or if we let them "fester like a sore." We examined whether or not we carried them around constantly "like a heavy load," or if we let them spoil and "stink" up our whole lives. Or did we let them "explode" and destroy everything around us? Then I assigned a five-paragraph essay for homework, asking students to write about a dream of theirs which they'd had to defer. Since they might be of a very personal nature, I said they would not have to share these pieces in class.

At the beginning of Tuesday's class I collected their essays and we moved on to Dickenson's "A Bird Came Down the Walk." Following our class discussion, I assigned a one page reader response, in which students were asked to write about some reaction they had to the poem. These papers would be shared in class.

The next day, Wednesday, we went around the room with each student reading aloud their responses. When I got to Lucy she glanced at me briefly and began to read. She started talking about a dream she'd had to defer and I remembered she had been absent from class the day before, but in an obvious effort to participate she was reading her Monday's homework assignment. I have never been more proud of a student, nor more on the verge of tears, than I was listening to Lucy share her dream of having her parents together.

The next day I learned even more about Lucy and her self-perception. The question of the day was, *If you could wake up tomorrow morning with a skill or quality you do not now have, what would it be.* Lucy's response was, "I'd like to be able to read and write better." I replied, "Really?" She said, "Yeah, sometimes I feel like people wonder why I can't do better than I do." I said, "Interesting. Do you want to get better enough to work with me some after school?" She said, "Yes" so I suggested we start that afternoon.

I began our after school session with this question: "Lucy, this morning you mentioned thinking 'other people' wonder why you don't do better than you do; do you think I wonder why you don't do better?"

After thinking a moment she responded, "Yeah, I guess I do, a little bit."

Then *I* thought for a moment and replied. "Lucy, when I was your age my mother was always there when we got home from school. She fixed supper for us every night. She checked on homework and made certain it got done. She made sure we went to bed at a reasonable hour and got us up in the morning with enough time to get ready for school. She made our breakfast and got us out the door in time to catch the bus. She did this every day. Does that sound like your life?"

"Uh, not even close."

"Lucy, I don't wonder why you don't do better than you do; I wonder how you do as well as you do."

This column originally appeared in Foster's Daily Democrat, Dover, NH on April 24, 2008.

There's an Essay in There Somewhere

The first paper my seniors have to write every year is a five to seven page personal narrative, though this coming year I'm thinking about adding in an earlier college essay. The paper is always open topic, the only restrictions being that the paper needs to be "school appropriate" and I don't want to read about illegal activities. However, even with that much freedom you have no idea, unless you're a teacher, how many times I hear the complaint—every year—"I don't know what to write about."

"What do you mean you don't know what to write about? You can write about anything that has happened in your life!"

"Nothing has happened to me."

"Nothing at all," I retort, "You wake up every day and never make it out of bed. You have no television, no friends, and no family. You don't cook, eat, work, or shop. You have no pets, prized possessions, dreams, or goals. You've never been on vacation, gone to a party, or had a sleep-over. You lie or sit all day every day in a permanent vegetative state."

"Well, yeah, but . . . nothing interesting, not that anybody would want to read about."

"I see," I continue. "You don't come to school every day? You've never had a class you really liked or really hated? You've never eaten in the cafetorium, never had an argument, never screwed up anything—never? Gee, I guess you don't exist, do you? You're just a figment of my overactive, highly caffeinated imagination, huh?"

"No, but I mean there's nothing I could write about that would give me five to seven pages."

"Okay, I'll tell you what—you come in for a conference and we'll find you a topic. We'll pick apart your life for a while—somewhere in there there's an essay, I guarantee it. Once we do that, the five to seven pages will take care of themselves." It always works.

I conferenced with a student once who had "absolutely nothing" to write about—nothing that would make a topic for a personal narrative. Well, during the conversation I discovered he had been collecting baseball cards for years, and had amassed quite the collection. "Hello! None of my students have ever written about baseball cards. I would love to read an essay about your collection." Guess what? It was a very fine essay.

I've had students write about their jobs, their pets, their parents, and their problems. One very shy young lady wrote about having to wear a pink tutu for an Upward Bound group presentation. Another wrote about an old hymnal that sat for years on her grandmother's piano. Michelle wrote about scooping ice cream at Friendly's and Kevin wrote about moving up through the color coded coats-of-rank at Market Basket. Ryan wrote about losing a play-off football game—one they *knew* they were going to win—and Corey wrote about what it was like to have an aged grandparent move in with you.

I've read essays about friends who have died tragically and who have lived tragically, about stuffed animals and stuffing a turkey. I've read about the birth of a talent, the birth of a niece and the birth of a cow. I've read essays on graveyards and junkyards. I've even read essays on writing essays. The possibilities are almost limitless.

The problem my students often have is that they look for some monumental, Earth shattering type event. It doesn't have to be that. Sometimes the dippiest little things can launch you into the neatest pieces of writing, like my grandson eyeing the yellow stickers they put on new blacktop before painting and saying one time, "Grampa, look, why did they put cheeses in the road?" Or the time my nephew asked my wife, "Aunt MaryAnne, how many people sleeps in your bed?" She replied, just your Uncle Stephen and me, why? He then asked, "How come ya gotz nine pillows?" They may be yet unwritten, but there are essays in there.

Last week MaryAnne and I were in the Nashville area visiting with her family, most of the time being spent with her sister Peggy and brother-in-law Garry. As always when we're together there was a lot of reminiscing. For example, I love this one. They once had a dog that was afraid of most men. It was a full-grown Terrier of some sort named Benji. Anyway, Peggy was sitting in a chair holding Benji so I thought that would be a good time to help the dog figure out I wasn't going to hurt him. I approached them slowly and spoke soothingly as I reached out to pet him. Poor thing, he just sat in her lap and shivered from fright as I continued to gently run my hand along his back . . . until I heard Peggy say, "Oh, oh," and she had to go change her clothes.

One day we got to talking about the jar of Avon skin cream she keeps in the car. When MaryAnne asked about it she said that she was trying to keep her skin from "looking like crepe paper." Then at some point we got to talking about the years they lived in Clarksville, TN, near the Fort Campbell, KY army base. Garry is a United Methodist pastor and he and Peggy were walking through their house one year just before their Christmas party, checking to be sure all was ready for the guests when they arrived. As Peggy walked by the crèche something caught her eye. Looking closer she saw that her four-year-old son had taken the baby Jesus out of the manger and replaced him with Darth Vader. No, it's not written yet, and I don't know exactly where it is, but there's got to be an essay in there somewhere.

This column originally appeared in Foster's Daily Democrat, Dover, NH on July 8, 2008.

Ready . . . Set . . .

One late August I'm getting ready for the start of school, and as usual finding myself saying, "where the heck did the summer go?" A couple of weeks ago it was a few days after graduation and my wife MaryAnne and I were headed to Nashville to visit with her family. Today it's Saturday and I am headed back to school on Monday. Wow!

The fact is I've already been in school over the last two weeks—quite a bit actually. A week ago I was in every day for a literacy workshop. This past week I've been in inventorying books, placing some last minute orders, attending a Teacher's Association breakfast for new teachers, and getting my "stuff" moved back into my room.

I kind of like the "moving back in" process, though. See when I get done my teaching responsibilities at the end-of-January semester break, there is still a lot to be done. I unload the bookcases, empty out one of the file cabinets, clean out my desk and the wardrobe/closet, pack up all the "stuff" in sturdy boxes to make way for the second semester teacher, and hide everything in a corner of a remote utility room. Then sometime after mid-summer, when the floors have been stripped and waxed and the tables and chairs returned, I move it all back in.

The good thing is I don't have the ability to accumulate the tons of materials, supplies, and "stuff" a lot of teachers do. The best thing, though, is I get to go through it all every time I unpack it, and relive some of my fondest teaching moments. There's the picture of me with Garry at his slightly belated graduation and the Heroes poster Adam's sister sent me after he died. There is the mini volleyball Meagan gave me, autographed by most of that year's team, and my Miracles jar filled with all kinds of sweet goodies. All of those things head back to their rightful place on my desk. Then there are the many cards and notes I've received over the years, which I just can't bear to toss: a note from Chuck and another from Betty congratulating me on my "new" column, Sheila's Christmas cards, so many senior pictures they will no longer fit on my picture bulletin board, quotes I've lifted out of student papers over the years; all those also find their way back into the proper desk drawer.

Then there are the weird, funny, and ridiculous things: Pictures of me as a six or seven-year-old at dance recitals—in full costume, pictures of my colleague Josh Tabor and me taken mid ride on a Busch Gardens roller-coaster, an old instamatic snapshot of Julie, Kenneth, and me from middle school, an autographed glossy of Carl Yastrzemski and me, from the eighties when I was in food service and he did promotional work for Kahn's hotdogs, a couple of my class pictures from Rollinsford Grade School, and the video and stills of my 1998 sky-dive. I pull those things out from time to time whenever I feel like my kids need a good laugh. And to a high school student, a picture of their teacher in a satin sailor suit with tap shoes, or as a slightly chubby eighth grader, or with cheeks pulled back from the wind force of a thirteen thousand foot free-fall is pretty funny.

Then I move over to my bookcase and start on those boxes. I pull out a number of books I had at UNH. I think of Tamara when I pull out Anne Lamott's *Bird by Bird*, and my old beat up copy of Tim O'Brien's *The Things They Carried*, the copy I still use when I teach it. I think of Les Fisher when I place all of my James Baldwin novels, as well as his complete collection of essays, on the shelf; *Sisters of the Spirit* brings forth my class with Lisa McFarlane, *Moby Dick* Briggs Bailey, and James Weldon Johnson's *God's Trombones* recalls one of my last literature classes—taught by John Ernest. I do this every year and every year I remember how indebted I am to these people and many more.

Yes, slowly and carefully I go through all of those things and find their rightful places in my desk or in the bookcase or file cabinet, usually the same places they've occupied since I've had them—I am so anal. Each one brings a thought, a smile, or a mental picture as it passes through my hands, and I find myself wondering what things I'll get this year to add to the stash, the senior pictures not yet taken or signed, the notes yet unwritten and the cards unsent, the new people to whom I'll become indebted. This year my seniors are headed to Washington, DC for the first time. That will surely produce some memorabilia. I wonder if I could get a part-time job with that Vitamin Water company and get an autographed picture with David Ortiz—or not. Maybe I'll get another mini volleyball this year, or maybe the football team will start tossing out mini footballs this year—I don't know.

I do know a few things, though. I know I need to check out what Anne Lamott has written that I haven't read, because I love her work. And I know I need to go shopping for my miracle jar and some new plants, as some of last year's didn't make it. I'm also thinking that my huge laminated poster of me in free fall at about ten thousand feet is fading a bit so maybe it's time for another sky-dive. And I definitely need to get another bulletin board for senior pictures, since the one I have ran out of space several years ago. Gosh, it's almost time to . . . go!

This column originally appeared in Foster's Daily Democrat, Dover, NH on September 9, 2008.

From the Class of 1975 to the Class of 2012

As I have previously mentioned, the first assignment I give to most of my classes, including my freshmen, is a personal letter to me. I tell them I want to know what their expectations are for the course and that I want to learn something about them. The following is my take-off on that assignment—my personal letter to this year's freshmen class.

Dear freshmen,

Thirty-seven years ago I was sitting where you are. I was a fourteen-year-old-in-an-unfamiliar-building-dealing-with-brand-new-teachers-scared-to-death freshman. I didn't know where to go or what to do for the first several days. I figured I was okay with my agriculture class since I'd been planting, tending, and harvesting gardens for most of my life. Being an American I assumed I could manage English, if I could find the room. But I worried a lot about Algebra, and I knew I was in trouble with History of the Non-Western World. I remember thinking, "What the heck does that mean anyway?" I didn't even know there *was* a western world let alone a non-western one. So what do we study, the northern, southern, and eastern worlds?" You think I'm kidding? Not on your life! The only thing I knew in the early days of that year was that I wanted to be in the Dover High School marching band more than anything else in the world—and with the help of then DHS principal Harvey Knepp, and Ken Bolduc's willingness to keep a bus going to Dover from Rollinsford, I was. But I was also some scared.

Now I know that all of you aren't scared, but some of you are. You're worried about homework, about fitting in, about looking right, and acting right. Your hormones are driving you nuts at times, and a new zit can ruin your whole day. You don't want to stick out but you don't want to be invisible either. Some of you don't want to be late for class and others of you don't want to go to class. Some of you have just moved into town and didn't want to. Some of you have had miserable experiences in other grades and other schools. Some of you are dealing with all kinds of personal troubles and don't want school adding to them. Some of you don't have enough money for a new ipod or video game. Some of you don't have enough money for lunch. How do I know all these things? Hey, I have trouble remembering what meetings I have scheduled for this coming week, but I remember thirty-seven years ago very well.

Of course, there are some of you who just exude self-confidence, never have trouble fitting in, always look and act just right so that your school experiences have always been nothing short of perfect. Well, you can stop reading, because I'm not writing to you—I'm writing to everyone else, the not always *good*, the once-in-a-while *bad*, and the sometimes *ugly*. You'll be okay. In a few days things will get easier and less confusing. They really will get better.

I can't tell you that high school work won't be difficult, demanding, and plentiful. You think adding and subtracting fractions was tough? Wait till you have to multiply and divide them. You think a one-to-two page book report was impossible? How about a one-to-two page thesis driven research paper with two-three outside sources, and constructed using proper MLA formatting and documentation? You will have to expand your knowledge about wind and the Beaufort Scale, about substance abuse, sexually transmitted diseases, self exams for various forms of cancer, politics, the Constitution, World War II, and economics. You'll be taught to balance your workload, your extra-curricular activities, and your checkbook. You'll have to graph and map, compare and contrast, jump and run. You'll probably strain your eyes, your writing hand, and your muscles. You'll carry ridiculously heavy textbooks for English, science, history, wellness, math, Spanish or French, and government.

Oh yes, we teachers will expect you to work hard in class. We will assign our homework. If you screw up enough we may have to give you a detention. But we'll also be there to applaud your correct solution to an equation, to publicly acknowledge your efforts on an essay or history report or science project. We'll cheer your team whether you win or lose. We'll laugh with you when you tell a good joke and we'll cry with you when your best friend, or grandparent, or pet dies. We'll lend you our shoulder when you need it and we'll give you our ear when you want it. We'll encourage you and keep your confidences. We'll assign hands-on projects and not just textbook chapters. We won't just study about the mechanics of roller coasters we'll have you build one. We won't just have you read the stories of other people, we'll teach you to write your own. We'll teach you to create language portfolios and stock portfolios, about the decimal system and the legal system. We'll seek out your thoughts and ideas and not just spout our own. We'll aggravate you, frustrate you, amuse you, and love you.

You think I know all these things just because I'm a teacher? I told you, I remember thirty-seven years ago. Not only did I manage to survive English, I learned to teach it. I didn't conquer the non-western world but I did learn what it was, and I was not only okay with Agriculture but eventually my horticulture class went to the FFA Nationals. I was a member of the Dover High marching band for all four years of high school and even algebra didn't cause me as much trouble as I thought it would. So come on—you can do it. I *know* you can. Just give us a chance. Give yourself a chance.

Grace & peace,
Mr. Mac

This column originally appeared in Foster's Daily Democrat, Dover, NH on September 23, 2008.

The New Year

I love new year's day. No, not the one on January 1st; I'm frankly not wild about that one—way too cold for me. I'm talking about the first day of the new school year. Yes, I usually leave the building a little hoarse but it is always a great day, and one I have looked forward to for weeks. This year was no exception; in fact it was maybe among the very best.

I have the coolest new batch of students this year: one block of Honors English IV (seniors), a block of English IV (again, seniors), and a block of Honors English II (sophomores). And one of the neatest things is that almost everyone was glad to be back at school and was looking forward to the new year. Oh yeah, I had a few who just wanted to crack jokes, another few who periodically cracked knuckles, and one who I think spent several minutes picking bellybutton lint, but they really are the coolest kids. Their first homework assignment let me know for certain just how cool.

Some years I start out with writing about a summer activity, while others, you may recall, I assign a personal letter to me in which I tell them I want to know their expectations for the course and to learn something about them. This year the letter won. The opening line of the first letter I read said, "I am very thrilled to have a chance to experience a class with you." What made that particularly special for me was that later in the letter this student said that her first encounter with me was when I happened to be sitting near her in the caf. . . "I was swearing during lunch and since your table was near you overheard and reprimanded me for it." I'm glad she didn't hold a grudge.

The thing I found impressive in another letter was the student knew he had a weakness; he also knew he had a strength—and wanted to share it. He admitted he was not wild about writing. "I love to read, though, so hopefully I will contribute to class discussions. I read very well and I am willing to read anything during class." That I should have such a problem student!

Another student admitted that socially "I tend to talk way too much, but when it comes to talking in class I'm not always up to par." Yet he planned to use our class to work on "becoming a better public speaker and have more confidence within [him]self." Still another stated, "I want to know what defines a good writer, what some of the traits would be. This semester I want to learn as much as I can in what little time we have and I want to be pushed to do better." What more could any teacher ask?

"One thing that would be great for the class would be the use of music as a mode of teaching," yet another wrote. "I know that you use music in your class [it's hard to miss my digital piano!] so I would love to see what you do with that as I am a massive music fan." Later in the letter he stated, "I hope that this year of English will be an incredible experience and will help me grow friendships with other students in my grade." Can you believe these kids?

One young lady wrote, "I want to become a more confident writer, to take pride in my work, and not be embarrassed about sharing it with my classmates and peers. Overall, I would like to improve my writing skills because I enjoy writing and I think it is a very good skill to have. Reading wise, I would like to increase my vocabulary level and I would like to read more fluently when reading out loud." Too bad she set her sights so low, huh?

There were several letters that also had their lighter moments. Two students commented on their strong faith in God and how much their religious beliefs had helped them grow. A couple spoke of their love of traveling, and a number wrote about their passion for sports and the influence athletics and coaches had had in their lives. Some mentioned their pets, others their pet peeves. One even wrote about her irrational fear of party balloons.

One of the more poignant letters came from a foreign exchange student who, half a world away, had left behind family and a lifetime of friends to spend her final year of high school here with us. She wrote, "This year I expect more from myself, and through your class I expect to improve my English skills, to be able to speak and to write more fluently, to be able to communicate more easily, and to become more aware of English literature . . . its history and its rules. However, my expectations are not only academic. I also expect to get myself new wings, to learn more about people and about myself, to believe in myself, in what I do and in how I think. I expect to find my way, to follow the light. I expect to change my life, to change the world, and that could just begin from here—from an English class." Nobody needs to tell this girl to dream big.

So this is my response to all you seventy some students who poured out your expectations to me, all you emerging public speakers, vocab builders, musicians, even my lint picker and my globophobe (yes, fear of balloons is a genuine phobia!): My first thought was, *Wow, I'm only one person! How can I hope to successfully address everything you expect?* But then I realized that for almost seven hours every weekday for the next five months I'm surrounded by you. How can I miss? Happy new year!

This column originally appeared in Foster's Daily Democrat, Dover, NH on September 15, 2009.

Interesting

The following is a short essay I wrote to my fall 2005 freshmen class. I came across it the other day and thought it appropriate to share it with you, with a name change or two. Consider it a tribute to a group of kids who will graduate this coming June and who changed my life along the way.

I'd been looking forward to the first day of the new school year, now some fifteen days old, for weeks. About 7 a.m. I went down to hook up with my sophomore friends, only to remember they'd become my junior friends, got a lot of high-fives, hugs, and the first MacKenzie/Ferland handshake of the year—you really ought to see this handshake! Then came my first two blocks of the day: Honors IV.

With some of these folks it was renewing old friendships and with others it was making new ones. We talked about the literature for the course, the major papers, Project Running Start, some upcoming special events and the ropes course field trip. Then came block three, the last stop of my teaching schedule: English I and a brand new crop of freshmen.

Don't get me wrong. I love freshmen—at least I try to. No, I do; I just have to work harder at it. No, even that's not right. It's easy to love them; it's just not always easy to teach them. They tend to make me a little . . . crazy.

My seniors come in most days all charged up and excited, even if I'm lecturing on the conventions of literary criticism. My freshmen come in most days looking about as excited and charged up as John Kerry did on election night 2000—a slight exaggeration, but you should see this bunch of kids. I have Mr.

Cosmopolitan, "Oh, New York City is the greatest place on Earth and I've been there." I have others who may never have left Somersworth. I have three or four whose mouths are direct wired to a wall socket, and three or four more who need a jump start just to croak out a lousy "hello." I have sharp dressers, casual dressers, and Jon, my punk dresser. They have black hair, brown hair, blond hair and red hair—Crayola crayon, magic marker, stop sign red! I have some who can't answer a question in less than a five-paragraph essay. I have others whose total vocabulary consists of *yup, nope,* and *I don't know*. This is going to be one interesting class.

My Miriam Webster's defines *interesting* as "holding the attention" or "arousing interest." My freshmen class defines *interesting* as Jon, for example, who sports a large, metal, inverted "U" in each ear and an attitude that vacillates between feigned indifference (I really know he cares about class) and not-so-passive aggressive. Or Rupin and Roy, who would drop dead before they'd be rude to me or not do a homework assignment, as opposed to say Chris, Tristan, or Ricco where I'd drop dead if they *did* do a homework assignment. There's Frank who doesn't shut up, Miss Vicki who won't open up, and Brianna who can't wake up. I've got Amanda the singer, Chelsea the jockette, Jessie the flirt, and Mikey the flirt-in-training. Then there's Johnny whose stock comment is "that's gay," the quiet and shy Nicole (quiet and shy with everybody but Jessie!), strawberry blonde Cory, and the studious Marie (who loves to write but "shh," don't tell anybody). I have "Cito" who rarely opens his backpack, and Jerry who never removes his backpack. I also have Anthony who doesn't like to be called Tony and who looks like Jon's hair if he has to talk in class, and tiny Brittany who almost gets lost in her chair. Then there's David. What does one say about David? He's not too big, or too small, or loud, or quiet, or motivated, or lazy. I guess he's just . . .

just. He's like ordinary, middle-of-the-road average. He's just a regular kid. Gee, go figure—I actually have one of those.

I guess there's probably some "regular" in a bunch of them. Even at that, though, they still "hold my attention"! Like yesterday, Roy actually shared his piece in class, out loud. I barely had to ask, and his lip didn't even quiver—but mine did a bit. The other day every single student in class read when it was their turn. And you'll never believe this one, there are only three or four who haven't written a draft of their personal narrative. We've learned that Mikey loves to play hockey, and at least he thinks he's good at it. And while Miss Vicky may rarely share her inner feelings her outer smile is something else. Yeah, they all have their quirks and some of them are bigger quirks than others, but none are really terrible. I guess if I threw 'em all into a big jar and shook it up they'd look pretty much like . . . David: kind of regular.

"Interesting" or "regular," who's to say? I mean New York is a pretty exciting place. And get this, yesterday Anthony told me I could call him Tony. Maybe Mikey really is good at hockey. So what if Jessie does flirt a little with Nicole? They do look kind of cute together. And, who knows, maybe someday there'll be a MacKenzie/Clark handshake, and maybe Tristan will do his homework. Maybe Jerry will take off his backpack and Johnny will decide "that's straight." Maybe I can get Brianna to drink coffee—lots of heavily caffeinated coffee. Maybe Jon will wear a dress shirt and tie. Maybe I'll try red hair—or not! Regular or "interesting." I've no doubt it'll all work out. Still, the next time Miriam Webster revises their dictionary, they ought to come visit my class first.

This column originally appeared in Foster's Daily Democrat, Dover, NH on March 24, 2009.

Around the World (Every 180 Days)

It occurred to me again yesterday, as I sat down with a couple of my department members after school, that I work with some incredible people. We were trying to pull together some material as evidence for the annual New England Association of Schools and Colleges (NEASC) report that Sharon Lampros, our building principal, must submit in order to maintain our accreditation. Some of us were meeting, some of us were emailed information, some of us dropped off hard copies of classroom materials and assignments. The point is we were all working together to get the job done. Within twenty minutes or so, save for one or two things I needed to find and copy, we had everything compiled and ready to get down to Sharon—amazing!

That task, made brief by working together, caused me to think about each member of my department and even more about how lucky I am to have such incredible colleagues alongside me every day. Now mind you, I have all kinds of concerns about the whole NEASC accreditation process, but pulling together that material gave me one more opportunity to converse with, to learn from, to appreciate my fellow department members. The really amazing thing, however, is that my appreciation does not stop with the departmental work or responsibilities. I think maybe the trip just begins there.

As I was leaving the building I noticed an Amnesty International poster on the wall outside Matt's room. See a project in his debate class a couple of years ago led to the students becoming involved in the Save Darfur movement. That involvement eventually expanded into an affiliation with Amnesty

International through which some of those same students, now far removed from the debate class, continue to raise both funds and awareness of human rights issues around the globe. Wow! All that from a debate over whether the situation in Darfur really is a civil war or genocide, and whether or not the United States has a right to inject itself into the struggle . . . or a responsibility to do so.

Continuing to make my way out of the building I saw Jackie, one of our most up-to-date technology gurus. I asked her for a copy of a pod casting assignment she did with her seniors, which she gave me the next morning. You should have heard the pod casts her students did during her *Night* unit. She doesn't just think about herself and her own students either. Do you have any idea how much easier the field trip to Washington, D.C. last October was because she helped me put the whole thing together? Jackie is still in her first full year at Somersworth, but she has become such an active and vital member of the faculty that most of us can hardly remember when she wasn't here.

Then there is Cait who is just developing this incredible reputation with her students. You should have seen the "banquet" her class invited me to a couple of years ago, officially hosted by the Maycomb citizens of *To Kill a Mockingbird*, in full costume. She also is the junior class advisor and you ought to watch one of their weekly meetings; those kids look like they're having so much fun it almost makes me want to join! Then there was the mini Renaissance Fair last fall—Cait organized it almost single-handedly. I can hardly wait to see what she does for the full blown all-school fair this coming May.

A few steps later and I was in front of Jimmy's room. Jimmy is sort of the patriarch of our "family." You would not even believe how many students register each year for his Intro to Philosophy classes. I'm not sure if they get more from the philosophers of ancient Greece or from the philosophies they adopt on their own, but it might just be the most popular elective in the entire building. The other class he teaches that kids love is poetry. Some years he does an all-class display of their work. The students will have their work posted in various creative and artistic ways for viewing, and they are with it for questions and comments. It's really a great tribute—both to them and Jimmy.

Just as I was about to turn the corner of the stairway I looked down the hall to the last room of the English wing, home of Donna, and I'm reminded of the final exam project she does with her Honors English III classes: a dinner-theater/murder mystery. It is totally student driven, drawing on the characters from their literature, and nothing short of amazing how they script it, plan it, and execute it. She also serves as the advisor to the National Honor Society.

Do you see what I mean? Yes, I have some awesome students, so does every other teacher in the school, but I also have some awesome colleagues, and we go to some amazing places. Some of them are literal, some of them are figurative, but they're all pretty special. We've traveled to the pre-civil rights south with Jem, Scout and Atticus and to the Mississippi Delta with Huck Finn. We've traveled to Germany and Eastern Europe on a trip narrated by Ellie Wiesel. We've been to Tolstoy's Russia, Mahfouz's Egypt, O'Brien's Vietnam, and our very own national capitol. Through poetry we've scoured much of the world (and through paperwork much of New England for NEASC!). The trips have been utterly incredible, whether we were riding on sheets of paper, the pages of literature, or the seats of a coach bus. And you know what the coolest part is? We get to do it again next year!

This column originally appeared in Foster's Daily Democrat, Dover, NH on February 24, 2009.

PART II

THE MAKING OF A TEACHER

I was admonishing a student one day in early December that I thought he was working too much. I had asked him point blank how many hours a week he was putting in at his job and he admitted it was over thirty. I looked at him and shook my head.

"I don't think that's very healthy for you at this point in your life, do you?" I queried.

"Well, staying warm at night is pretty healthy," he responded.

A student asked me one day if he could possibly come to my house to do a load of laundry, because he was totally out of clean clothes and their washing machine had broken down and they didn't have the money to get it repaired. He didn't even have enough money to go to the laundromat.

I think it was a Monday and my question of the day was, share something with us that one of your parents did that made you proud of him or her. One student said, "I'm proud of my dad because he almost never misses one of my games." Another said, "I'm proud of my mom for the way she takes care of me and my brothers and sister." Still another said, "I'm proud of both of my parents for how hard they work to provide a home for us." Then one student said, "I'm proud of my mother for quitting drinking."

I was in a meeting one time with an administrator and a student who had problems. I had the student in class; I really liked him and he liked me, but that didn't keep him out of trouble. During our conversation he looked at his watch and remarked that he had to get going because his mom had told him to come right home after school and go straight to his room. I asked if he was in trouble with her as well and he said, "No, but she said that when she and her boyfriend got home they might want to fool around in the living room and they didn't want me in there."

There are so many things intricately associated with being a teacher that just aren't taught from a textbook or a university classroom. Some things just have to be learned by experience. And how you deal with them determines what kind of a teacher you will become. You may become a teacher who kids respect, value, trust, even love. Or you may just become a teacher.

Settling to Be a Teacher

I was listening to a student one time talk about a friend he thought was selling himself short, because after all, this friend had the ability to "do anything he wanted," yet was "settling for teaching." We were talking about teaching in one of my classes recently, about how important teachers are and the enduring value of what they do, but also, as the kids noted, what they have to "settle for" in terms of compensation and image. Based on some of the stereotypes they raised, they weren't entirely wrong: *you'll never get very far on a teacher's salary* or *teachers only work part-time anyway,* or the old standby, *those who can do, and those who can't teach.* Thank goodness most of us in teaching don't think much about that kind of talk.

At some point during the conversation I was asked why I "settled" for being a teacher. I looked at them intently and said, "What are you talking about, settling? I have the best job in the world!"

"How do you figure that?" they responded.

"Listen, today is a Monday and I couldn't wait to get to school. The sun is shining, I'm here doing something I love with people I love, and getting paid to do it. You guys, life doesn't get any better than this!"

I'm not sure they totally believed it but I could tell it got some of them thinking. It got me thinking: about a senior named Seth I'd had my first year at Somersworth, who told me that he was pretty sure he was going to do something that would make a lot of money, but that eventually he knew he would become a teacher. We met up for coffee a few months ago so he could ask me about the certification process. I also had Ryan that year, a history teacher at Winnicunnet, and Mike who is teaching in York. A few years later I had Katelyn.

Katelyn was a member of the Class of 2002, one of the most motivated classes I've had the privilege of teaching. Among the top ten there was Chris, who graduated from Dartmouth and is an investment banker in San Francisco, James, who is in his first year of medical school in Florida, Kevin who is with a high powered information technology firm in Massachusetts, Alex, who was a senior at Clarkson majoring in mechanical engineering and habitually on the Dean's List prior to his accidental death, Jamie, a product specialist for a major manufacturing firm, Pete, whose group's business plan took 1st place in one of his classes and who currently serves on the Somersworth School Board, and I could go on. Not to forget Katelyn, 5th in her graduating class, member of a championship volleyball team and of the basketball 1000 point club, she went to Boston College to major in . . . yes, secondary education. A couple of years ago I learned that she was having a tough few days, so I gave her a call just to say, "hi, I'm sorry," and "hang in there—I believe in you." A few days later I got the following note from her:

9/26/04

Mr. Mac,

It was so nice to hear from you today! I just think of how lucky I am, and all the others who have passed through the doors of SHS, to have you in their lives. It really is a blessing. I was sitting with my friends when you called and they thought it was such a wonderful thing to have such a caring teacher. It reminded me of graduation and the overwhelming feeling of inspiration, gratitude, and love I had for the teachers in my life. I think of you, Mrs.

Turgeon, Ms. Nadeau and I just have to smile. I hope and pray that I bring the same caring atmosphere to my classroom and teaching career.

Miss you, see you soon!

Love,
Katelyn

Teaching is not a "fallback position." It's not a high profile, high powered executive job. Around here it takes several years just to reach mid five figures. Six figures? Not in my lifetime. No, teaching is not any of those things, it's just incredible. In general, the best teachers can't do anything else. It's not that they're not able to do anything else—they *can't* do anything else. They might claim it's their mission, their calling, their passion, but whatever you label it, they *can't* do anything else. And if they could they probably should, because they'll not likely ever really make it as a teacher. They won't experience the thrill of a student finally mastering a successful essay conclusion. They won't hold a sobbing kid following a playoff loss or the death of a friend. They won't see the hidden smile on the face of a hard working special-ed student who typically gets D's but just pulled off a B- on a test. They won't offer comfort and support to the student whose parents are divorcing or who gets caught cheating and the remorse is nearly unbearable. They won't smile when a student introduces them to their mother, and then tear up from overhearing as they walk away, "Is that one of your teachers?" "Nope, he's just always really nice to me."

All those former students I mentioned a few lines ago? I have cell numbers and email addresses for all of them and countless dozens more from over the years. And every once in a while I call, or they call, or we email. Sometimes we get together for volleyball.

On breaks and vacations we may meet up for breakfast or lunch. I made a copy of that note from Katelyn and I sent it to her the other day with a note of my own, which along with some other things said this: "you will bring that same caring atmosphere, and much more, to your classroom and teaching career—because you *can't* do anything else.

Settling? Are you kidding me?

This column originally appeared in Foster's Daily Democrat, Dover, NH on January 4, 2007.

Where Are the Parents?

The question gets asked every school day. It gets asked respectfully, angrily, pleasantly, and rhetorically. It gets asked when kids are truant, when they're failing, when they're cutting class, when they're being suspended. It gets asked when a teacher is dealing with a classroom behavior issue or when a paper is plagiarized. It gets asked when a student is sick or injured. Sometimes it gets asked when an IEP meeting is scheduled to begin. It often gets asked at the end of parent conference nights: Where are the parents?

Well, teaching has taught me a few things about parents and parenting—maybe even more than being a parent and grandparent did. I know, for example, that there are many reasonable answers to that question. Parents are working, trying to keep mortgages and rents current, food on the table, clothes on their kids, and automobiles running. They're getting kids to practices, rehearsals, doctors and dentists, church, confirmation classes, and afterschool jobs. When my brothers and I were kids our mother was virtually a one-woman taxicab company, and she didn't have to work outside the home!

Parents aren't just working either. They're helping with homework and projects. They're trying to make time for dinners, movies, fishing trips, ball games, and vacations. Many of our parents serve as coaches, assistant coaches, score keepers, and time keepers. They sell candy, tickets, and raffles at games. They sit on ridiculously hard, uncomfortable benches to watch plays and concerts, or on freezing cold bleachers to see a football or hockey game. They rise early to get them up and stay up late to see them in. They check homework, eyes, and breath. Most parents want to raise good kids.

Does that mean there are no bad parents, that none of our parents set bad examples with substance abuse, living arrangements, language, and discipline? Clearly it doesn't mean that. We've had parents come to school under the influence of alcohol. We've had to remind parents that they can't smoke on school grounds. We've listened to parents yell, swear, and threaten (us and their kids). What I have come to understand and appreciate, though, is that when we are frustrated enough with a student to call the parents, typically the parents are pretty frustrated too. I'm not sure we consider that enough. Face it; we at school don't want to be in constant difficulty with a student, so we look to the parent for help and support. Well, most parents don't want to be in constant difficulty with their kids either, so they sometimes look to the school for help and support. It makes sense if you think about it, so maybe we should think about it more.

I've dealt with a lot of parents since I've been a teacher, and a few of them have been lousy parents and lousier role models. Some I've even thought should be arrested for abuse or neglect—or just plain idiocy. But they were a tiny minority. I can't tell you how many parents of my students have been thrilled to get a call, a letter, or a note from me telling them how well their child is doing, or how much I'm enjoying having them in my class. I can't tell you how many have called or written me to express thanks for a deadline extension, for helping their son or daughter after school, for giving them a ride home, or for just being what they thought was a positive influence.

I'll never forget Johnny, who was suspended once for several days. I knew his short-term retention was not great so I called mom to see if I could come to their home and give him a test he'd missed, which I did. A couple of years later I heard this voice say, as I was buzzing through Market Basket, "I don't remember your name but I know you're Johnny's teacher." I turned and saw a familiar smiling face. "I don't remember your name either but I know you're Johnny's mom." She was one of my parents.

I was sitting in the bleachers with my friend and former student, John, one day last semester watching his brother, Bobby, one of my current students, play basketball. As I often do I asked how his folks were. He pointed across court to the scorekeepers table and said, "There's my dad, over there." He is one of my parents.

Some years ago I had a student sitting on the other side of my desk one day after school. He was dealing with a significant drug abuse problem and asking for my help.

"Do you trust me?" I queried.

"Of course," came the reply.

"Do you trust your mom?"

"Yes."

"Do you love your mom?"

"Absolutely."

"I think we need mom's help with this."

I called that evening and the next afternoon the three of us were sitting in my room trying to find some solutions to his problems. She was one of my parents.

Early in the first semester one year I had a parent stop me as I was leaving a volleyball game. "Mr. MacKenzie, I'm Brianna's mother. I want you to know how much she loves being in your class. She feels comfortable in your room and talks about you and your class all the time." She was one of my parents.

I have conferenced with parents in their homes, in my home, at school, over the phone, and through emails. Sure, I've had a few unpleasant exchanges over the years, but they are the exceptions. Where are the parents? Mine are keeping stats at basketball games and trying to help their kids with drugs and allowing me to give tests in their living rooms and passing along positive feedback and . . . trying to be the best parents they can be.

This column originally appeared in Foster's Daily Democrat, Dover, NH on March 27, 2008.

Failing

Did you ever get an F in school? Well I did. It wasn't in high school—the lowest grade I ever got there was a D and I only received one of those. Of course you were probably one of those brainy kids who always did the right thing, always studied, always behaved like a perfect angel, and who truthfully the rest of us could hardly stand. Well I admit it; I did get an F in college. *In what?* you ask. In English 401. Yes, folks, I am an English teacher who failed freshman English at UNH—in 1976—twenty years before I graduated with high honors.

A few years after I started teaching I had a freshman, Kyle, who failed my English I class. I tried everything I could to motivate him. We did "open topic" journal writes so he could focus on things important to him. Living only a few doors from my house he would occasionally drop by with a friend or two, just to chat. I never put him off and always steered the conversations away from his burdens at school. At the end of the course I offered to give him an "incomplete," rather than the "F" he'd actually earned, if he would work with me to finish the course during the second semester. Sadly, he still failed.

Believe it or not, failing was the topic of my commencement address to the Class of 1998. Maybe not my brightest move ever, but, yes, I talked to more than a thousand people, many of them the folks who pay my salary, about my having once failed freshman English—and survived. I also talked about a job I once applied for, one I had been essentially assured of based on the job I'd done as interim. I failed to be the successful candidate. Several years later I found myself writing a letter of recommendation for a graduating senior, talking as much about his failures as his successes.

The letter was for Chris. He took practically every honors course Somersworth High offers, registering for Advanced Placement Calculus and Advanced Placement English Language and Composition his senior year. I don't recall his GPA but I do recall he was valedictorian of his class. Chris was also actively involved with class leadership and was a gifted athlete, excelling in not one sport but three! Yet when one looked a bit deeper than the athletic stats, the transcripts, and the GPA another picture began to take shape. He was in some ways quite the failure.

During Chris's senior year something like half of the players on his struggling basketball team quit half-way through the season—not Chris. As captain he set the example for those who stayed; you don't bail because you lose some games. This is the same dedication and loyalty Chris brings to the classroom. In the preceding year Chris had been dealt perhaps an even bigger blow. After being class president for his first two years he lost the election for junior year. That's not "the rest of the story," though, because Chris stuck right in there with the other class officers and leaders and worked at least as hard as he did when he was president. I was proud to write in his letter of recommendation that "Chris handled the loss of his two-year class presidency with a grace and dignity worthy of any politician's emulation."

Here's the thing about failures. They are at least as valuable to our human development as successes, maybe more, if we learn from them. My failing English 401 taught me that when I did it again I needed to work—and I pulled an A- the second time around. My interim year as a summer camp director taught me that I really wanted to work with kids and teach. I've just finished my tenth great year at Somersworth High.

Chris? Oh, he learned, too. In his valedictory speech Chris talked about what it took to achieve success, the hard work, focus, and determination. He quoted Vince Lombardi's belief that "any man's finest hour, the greatest fulfillment of all that he holds dear, is that moment when he has worked his heart out in a good cause and lies exhausted on the field of battle." Then Chris spoke of his own belief that winning isn't all skill, brains, or muscles. Rather, "true winners, true champions are created by getting knocked down." More importantly, "life's truest test is how you get back up." After his four grueling years I sat on the town common in Hanover, NH and watched Chris receive his diploma from Dartmouth.

Kyle also took some lessons from his experiences with me and English I. No, they were probably not in the areas of college prep or constructing a well organized five-paragraph essay or offering detailed responses to questions on John Steinbeck's *Of Mice and Men*. Yet I know he took away something of value because last summer he sat on my back porch with a friend and said, "Hey, Mr. MacKenzie, I'm wicked excited. I have you again for English I—you're my favorite teacher!" I looked over at the friend and said with a grin, "This from a man who failed my class—how does that work?"

From the serious over-achiever, who never had to work so hard to graduate college, to the severe under-achiever, who will have to work three times harder just to graduate high school— they each have had their successes and failures. Something else this Dartmouth graduate and Somersworth High School repeating freshman have in common is, they help make people like me become better teachers. I can't just teach to the middle—I have to reach the ends, too. Yes, UNH stamped *Magna Cum Laude* on my diploma, but the Chrises and Kyles of Somersworth High School bring it to my life.

This column originally appeared in Foster's Daily Democrat, Dover, NH on July 12, 2007.

Books in the Buff

The headline, *Bodies and books not naughty at all*, had caught my eye even before I opened Tamara's email letting me know about Jason Claffey's article in last Thursday's *Foster's* on the new Rollinsford Public Library. I knew about the project from head librarian Tamara Neidzolkowski herself, as she had recently shown me the calendar featuring twelve plus almost nude Rollinsfordians—but only after I promised to buy one once they were delivered. Fighting for tax dollars, like most municipal entities these days, the library meets much of its budget through fundraisers, and I hope they make a ton of money with this one.

I first met Tamara Neidzolkowski in January of 1994 when she was my English 401 instructor at the University of New Hampshire. I don't have any idea why I took to her as I did. She taught English 401, which I was only taking because I had earned an AF (Administrative Failure, for failing to attend class!) eighteen years earlier. She assigned us an eight to ten page research paper; I hadn't written anything longer than a one-page letter in almost twenty years. She wanted MLA formatting and documentation; I didn't even know what that meant. She was a classic liberal living in the world of academia; I was a semi-conservative Republican from the world of business. I should have known better. I didn't.

I had gone to UNH to do a degree in music, yet after one or two sessions of Tamara's English 401 course I switched my major to English. Maybe it was because Tamara sat *on* the desk not *at* it or because she questioned administrative and academic policies, and encouraged us to do the same. Maybe it was because she didn't fear the outlandish, like people who questioned the moon landing or the JFK "magic bullet" assassination. She broke nearly every model of "teacher" I'd ever known.

Tamara was certainly unconventional. When we'd ask her about whether or not she ever wanted to have children she said something like, "Oh, I might decide to squeeze out one or two some day." She was the first teacher I remember who cared more about the content in her students' papers than the construction. She was the first teacher I ever remember who was more concerned *that* her students thought than with *what* they thought. She was also the first teacher I ever heard drop an F bomb in class!

Tamara is definitely why I teach English. My wife, MaryAnne, had been a teacher all of her adult life and loved it. I got nauseous just thinking about it. Yet, I distinctly remember thinking to myself after that first or second English 401 class, "Wow! If I could teach like that, I could teach."

So I became a teacher. I have to spend more time on mechanics than she did. I can't swear in class never mind drop F bombs, and I'd probably get flack from parents and my principal if I talked much about *squeezing out* babies. But I can encourage them to *think*. I encourage them to think about their education, the politicians they support, the things they do to their bodies, how they use their money, supporting their school, caring for their families. I encourage them to write, to read, and to use the library—their school library and their public library. I encourage them to *think* about planning for babies before they start making them. Maybe more than anything I encourage them to love and value themselves, because if they can't do that everything else is a waste. Much of this stems from of what *I* got out of my English 401 course at UNH some fifteen years ago.

Today, not much surprises me about Tamara Neidzolkowski. It doesn't surprise me that each year she's still willing, even eager, to come into my classroom and do a guest spot kicking off my seniors' eight to ten page research paper. It doesn't surprise me that she's as in-tune and passionate as ever about all the major issues of the day. It doesn't surprise me that this career woman would become a stay-at-home mom for her two children. It doesn't surprise me that this person who once worked at a university with a student population of over ten thousand would make it her mission to bring a public library to a town of less than three thousand. It doesn't surprise me that she invited my students to come do a children's reading, nor does it surprise me that they accepted. A teacher at heart and a prolific reader herself, I can think of no better calling for Tamara than to be a librarian, to be instrumental and involved in both the academic and intellectual growth of a whole town—even if making her budget requires selling a calendar which features nude readers, and very classy nude readers by the way!

Speaking of that, you'll have to excuse me. I need to get to Mr. Mike's in Rollinsford, or someplace that's still open, to buy my calendar and support that new library. You may recall I promised I would when Tamara agreed to the preview. I laughed when she first handed me the draft copy, and I said with excitement, "Hey, am I going to get to see you naked?" She laughed and said, "No, I'm not in it . . . but my husband is." *"Great,"* I replied, a tad sarcastically. Anyway, I'm off for my purchase and then home to do some of my own reading—with my clothes on. You know, it's too bad we didn't have a public library in Rollinsford when I was growing up there in the 60s and 70s. Maybe I wouldn't have been an adult before I learned to appreciate reading. Of course I'm pretty sure a calendar with naked people on it would have helped, too. And to think—I almost majored in music.

This column originally appeared in Foster's Daily Democrat, Dover, NH on November 3, 2009.

A Defining Moment for Me

We were talking in class one day about topics for personal narratives—what things make good topics and what things don't. For example, I always suggest staying away from boyfriends and girlfriends, mostly because "nobody else is going to feel the way you do about your boyfriend or girlfriend." I also suggest they stay away from illegal activities, "because I don't want to know about them. And I'd like you to avoid the big game, since they all tend to sound the same. Best friends, on the other hand, or prized possessions, and *defining moments* tend to make excellent topics for personal narratives."

"So what's a defining moment," I was immediately asked.

"It's an event in your life that has really helped shape or define the person you have become, or perhaps the employee or sibling or student you have become."

"Can you give us an example?" someone queried.

I think for a moment and say, "Yeah, I can."

I was in the fourth grade at Rollinsford Grade School and whenever we finished our work for the day we were allowed to work on SRA folders till the bell rang. The SRA program was a series of readings followed by questions. Each one was an individual folder in this big box. They were organized alphabetically and by difficulty. This particular day I remember working in S's. All at once I heard my number called and realized I was about to miss the bus—and I lived too far away to walk. I stuffed papers and pencils into my desk, crammed my SRA folder into the box, and flew out the door.

The next morning something was buzzing around the room about our teacher being really mad, because someone had brought in a snake, knowing she was wicked afraid of snakes. Who would do such a dumb thing and to deliberately scare the teacher? No, someone had not actually brought in a snake, but had drawn a picture of a snake and put the picture on the teacher's desk. And they had done that just to scare her, because everyone knew she was afraid of snakes. No, no, not on her desk, on the SRA box, which she had to walk right by in the morning. Everyone wanted to know who'd done it, including me, though I remember wondering, who would be scared of some homemade picture of a snake anyway. I mean how scary could the picture be drawn by a fourth grader? Finally the teacher got up to speak.

"I am very upset that one of you would put that picture of a snake right where I couldn't miss it, knowing how frightened I am of snakes."

Wow! They were right, she *was* scared of a picture of a snake. Silence. Some sideways glances but not one word. Shoot, I had no idea she was afraid of snakes, and I still didn't know what the heck she was talking about.

"Now I don't know who did this but I do know it was one of the last of you to leave yesterday or I'd have seen it then."

Still not a word. "If you don't confess there will be trouble when I do find out who it was." I knew I had brought in no pictures of snakes so I had nothing to worry about.

"OK, take out your science books—we'll deal with this more later."

Just before morning recess we came back to it. "All right, people, if I don't hear from one of you by recess time there will be no recess." Nothing. "I want to know which one of you found that SRA folder with the picture of the snake on the cover; took it out of its proper alphabetical place, and stuck it in the very front of the box—just to scare me!"

As I heard this latest version of the mystery, realization began to unfold . . . working in 'S' section . . . rushing to catch bus . . . stuffed SRA folder in the front of the box . . . not its proper spot . . . Oh my gosh, it *was* me! But too much time had passed. She'd never believe I'd just figured out what she'd been talking about. I didn't do what she said. I mean I did it, but I didn't do it to scare her. I was in a hurry. I didn't know she was afraid of snakes. And it wasn't a real snake anyway, it was just a picture of a snake. Who's afraid of a picture? Who would admit they were afraid of a picture even if they were?

"I am going to give each of you a slip of paper. On it write your name and either 'I did it' or 'I didn't do it.' If I get an 'I did it,' you will all go out. If I don't, you won't. And we'll keep doing it every recess until one of you admits it."

I couldn't stand it. I wrote my name and 'I did it' on mine and passed it in. She began unfolding papers and eventually said, "OK, you may all go out."

Later she pulled me out into the hall and asked me why I had done it. No matter how much I tried to explain that at first I didn't understand and then I was scared—none of it mattered, because she didn't believe me anyway. She really thought that I had somehow devised this plot to scare her to death with an SRA folder. The punishment, when it came, never left: "Well, Steve, I guess you and I just aren't going to be friends anymore." And we weren't.

It was more than thirty years before I realized it, but that, folks, was a defining moment in what kind of teacher I have become.

This column originally appeared in Foster's Daily Democrat, Dover, NH on June 28, 2007.

Teaching What They Need

I don't know if other teachers think about this or not, but every once in a while I worry a little bit. Am I doing a good job? Am I giving my students what they need? Am I actually teaching them anything? I mean my goal always is to help my students be successful in my class and at the same time become more literate, better equipped to take their places in the larger society. But am I doing that? I mean I don't obsess over these things, but occasionally I slip and wonder if I'm really being effective, if I'm really giving them what they want, need, and deserve.

It's important to me that my students get at least part of what they're looking for or hope to get out of my class. Some students have told me they want to become better writers, while others claim they love reading and have heard we read some pretty good books in Honors English IV. There are always a few who state that they "want to get prepared for college English," or at the very least, "want to learn how to write college length papers." Some admit that they've heard my class will "teach [them] about life, not just English." Others will just come right out and say, "Mr. Mac, my friends have said they had a lot of fun in your class, so I want to have some fun."

My responses to them are probably about what you would expect. "I certainly hope you leave here prepared for your first college English class, since that is essentially what this course is. In fact, I patterned the class after my own English 401 course at UNH." Or, "You can plan on learning how to write longer papers, since all of your papers will be college length, from your 5-7 page personal narrative to your 8-10 page research paper with 8-10 sources, using proper MLA style (Modern Language Association) formatting and documentation." I have also responded, "Yes, Virginia, I hope we all learn a lot about life and how to more successfully participate in it." And "in everything we do I want you to have some fun; I certainly plan to. But bear this in mind; it is not essential we all come out of here having had the same exact experience. I want each of you to get what you need from this course."

I had a student one year who said, "I want to write better papers." *Okay,* I thought, *I can teach 'better' writing.* We were conferencing her personal narrative one day, which was about a girlfriend who had died, and I flagged a line in her conclusion that talked about the girl's mother who, up to her ankles in snow, sang at her daughter's graveside. "Right here you wrote 'She sang from the very depths of her heart.' First, that is a cliché and second, I have no idea what it means. It will mean something different to everyone. So *show* us what 'the very depths of her heart' looks like, what it sounds like." In her revised draft she wrote, "She sang as if she was not freezing in a cemetery at a funeral for her child. She sang as if Bitsy would have the chance to grow up, not like it was [her] last lullaby."

I had another student once who stated that he wanted to learn to write with more authority. I thought about it. *Yeah, I can teach 'authority' in papers.* Sometime early in his first semester at college he dropped me an email that went something like "Hey, Mr. MacKenzie, I wanted to let you know that one of my professors used my paper as an example of an essay where the writer had developed a clear, solid thesis statement. Apparently I was the only one in the class who had done so. I just wanted to tell you that, and say thanks for working us so hard."

Then there was the student I had as a sophomore in my public speaking course. As I recall she took the course because she wanted to learn how to speak in front of a class, or in public, with greater confidence. I remember thinking, *I can do 'confidence.'* I got an email from her a few weeks ago that among other things said, "... and I have to thank you! We did oral presentations in my Lit of the Ancient World class, and on my way to seminar the next day the professor stopped me to say that I had an excellent presence and speaking voice when I got up in front of people, and he was amazed to see it in someone so young. He also told me my group got one of the highest grades in the class because of me!"

Still, though, every once in a while you begin to question yourself—just the slightest bit of second guessing—at least I do. Like the other day when I was working with Brandon. Actually he was serving a detention—sort of—and I had him doing some make-up work. He was trying to crank out a short writing assignment and decided he needed to beat himself up some.

"You know, Mr. Mac, I'm just a pretty lousy writer, definitely not as good as most of the kids in the class."

I looked at him and said, "Okay Brandon, let's say that maybe you're not as strong a writer as *some* of the others. Why did you sign up for this course, what do you really want to get out of it?"

He looked at me for just a second and replied, "I want to be a better person."

I thought ... *Wow! How do I do 'better person'?*

This column originally appeared in Foster's Daily Democrat, Dover, NH on February 22, 2007.

My Bag of Tricks

There are lots of reasons why being a new teacher is tough. First of all you discover, in a sudden blitzkrieg of kids, that there is a huge difference between the theory of the university textbooks and the reality of the public school classrooms, and that you're a long way from the teacher's Hall of Fame. One day you're walking the paths of a familiar college campus headed for a cup of Chai and a whole wheat bagel, or more probably a beer with your friends, and the next you're in a strange building dealing with parents, colleagues, administrators, support staff, keys, phones, security codes, new computer software, and . . . kids, dozens of kids! For the first time you're *the* teacher—the encyclopedia, the dictionary, the expert, the hall monitor, the surrogate father or mother, the confidant, the captor, the purveyor of knowledge, the dispenser of discipline, the friend, the counselor—the enemy. Some of that trauma may be mitigated by an especially productive internship or student teaching experience, but it's still not the same. You've got to teach, and the biggest thing you lack is a bag of tricks.

No, I'm not talking about some hat from which you pull rabbits or doves or fake flowers. I'm talking about the figurative sack from which you pull the quick mini-lesson or talk-teaser, the minute mystery, the word game or incentive exercise, or any one of hundreds of short takes which can save both the class and your sanity. The bag of tricks is what you go to when you have nothing else to go to, when everything has fallen flat for the day, or when you have an extra ten minutes that can either unfold into a teaching moment or shrivel into utter chaos.

Now I haven't been a new teacher for quite some time but I never stop adding to my bag of tricks. It includes quotes as writing prompts, yes or no mysteries, a giant Scrabble board, my Wheel of Fortune/hangman game, trivia moments, all-aboard, the human knot, word games, and . . . you get the idea. But I'm still adding.

Last week I spent more than thirty hours in a five-day literacy workshop. We explored a lot of new ideas about integrating literacy into all our classrooms and recognizing that literacy is not confined to the English/language arts classes. We discussed what literacy instruction looks like in a science class, for example, and how that differs from how and what we would teach in an English class. We examined the various ways in which special education and language specialists would participate and support those efforts, but some of the best things I got out of the workshop were additions to my bag of tricks.

I loved the vocab cube where students have an actual cube on which they place a new vocabulary word. On the other sides of the cube will be a definition in the student's own words, a sentence using the word indicating their understanding of the definition, the part of speech, a synonym, and an antonym. Bet that kid's not going to forget that word in a hurry.

But that's not the only thing I added. There was the Predict-O-Gram for reading, more ideas for writing prompts, "T" Charts, and any number of other graphic organizers. One of the things I liked best was the Word Expert card. On a large index card I write a word from a given unit and text. The student will then add a visual representation or drawing of the word, the location of it in the text, its part of speech, and their own sentence. Throughout the unit the words will be put up on a section of wall in the classroom creating a "Wall of Words." Bet they won't forget those words either.

See a bag of tricks is essential for both teachers and students, every bit as necessary as learning to work with Power School (our computer grading system). It's as important as learning to hold your temper in check with a parent, or remembering your security code so you don't set off the burglar alarm when you come into school on the weekends. Let's face it, stuff happens. Lessons get finished early, get bogged down, or flop altogether. Discussions deteriorate. Computers crash. Fire drills break momentum. A student will suddenly loose it and take some of the class along with him or her. Some lesson you've planned is resulting in glazed eyes, yawns, and that deathly look of boredom. A teacher can't crash and burn. A teacher can't shut down shop. They can't take a break, call time out, yell, scream, or worst of all—cry.

A teacher has to teach, no matter what, and so the deeper the bag of tricks, the longer that list is and the more areas of instruction it covers, the better. There will be days—believe me— when your guest speaker doesn't show up or you look at your lesson plans five minutes before the start of a class and realize you've forgotten to reserve a TV or the computer lab or the library. The kids aren't going to forget to come to class—at least most of them aren't—and you can't look like an idiot. You've got to jot down that prompt for a journal write or come up with some small group discussion topics or find a substitute reading. And whatever you do it's got to be related to your current unit of study . . . or they'll know you've blown it. It's got to look like you planned it a week ago and you've got to execute it flawlessly. You better bet my bag of tricks is big and gets bigger with every workshop I take. I may never make it to stardom, but, who knows, my Wall of Words may help take one of my students to the Hall of Fame someday.

This column originally appeared in Foster's Daily Democrat, Dover, NH on August 19, 2008.

Doing My Best

I did a short journal write with my seniors this week. The prompt was the Buddha's last words of advice to his disciples: "Do your best." And so we wrote about doing our best, what that means and what it looks like. As we wrote my mind wandered a bit.

I had an Email response recently from a reader named Larry about a column I'd written. "Your column this week reminded me of a young man I had working for me when I was a graduate student. This kid was a total klutz, undisciplined, and had been passed from group member to group member, until I wound up with him. I was not exactly the most graceful virtuoso in the lab, so when he broke a vacuum line, I did not get mad, but told him how to get it fixed, and assigned him that task. When he made a mess of a distillation, I showed him a much easier and safer way of doing it. For some unexplained reason, this threw a switch in him. From then on he was my man Friday. The klutz mistakes stopped. He started doing some world-class research, and discovered a property of a new polymer I had synthesized that led to a patent, several publications, and which launched his career. He was pulling C's, D's, and F's up until then. He caught the fire and passion, and disciplined himself when he realized having the degrees might make people listen to him. He has spent his life since working in various university chemistry labs as an eternal postdoc, inventing new materials. He has compiled an impressive and prolific record few of the professor ranks can ever hope to match." Until he got paired up with Larry, the grad student was obviously not doing his best. Equally as obvious—neither were his

64

previous supervisors.

Then I was thinking about my student Joe. The day the concept papers (basically a brief synopsis) were due for our first major paper, a 4-6 page personal narrative, Joe did not have one. This set the memory bells a ringing. See I'd had Joe as a freshman and he refused early on to participate much in class. I urged, prodded, bribed, almost begged at times. Nope, nothing worked. Finally Joe admitted to me in a private conversation that he could not *stand* to be wrong in front of the class. He had simply chosen the safest way to avoid that possibility.

Determined to meet Joe's needs, I started working with him after school, just the two of us most days. We started out working on some very basic grammar worksheets: parts of speech, identifying clauses, those kinds of things. I remember that for several days we made progress. And I remember the day I blew it. I had gotten excited that he was doing well, so I pushed for a bit more, and then a bit more, and then a bit too much.

"I don't know," came the answer to the question.

"Sure you do, just remember what you did back here," I said pointing.

"So is it this?" he queried.

"No, look here again and you can figure it out," I nudged.

"I don't know. I can't do it," he said again.

"Yeah, you can, Joe, I *know* you can. Just give me your best shot."

We went back and forth like that for a couple of minutes until he finally exploded, exclaiming, "See, this is why I don't like to answer questions. I don't want to be *wrong*!" And he stormed out of the room, never to stay after school with me again. Clearly, I did not do my best.

So when Joe didn't have his concept paper I got concerned and went looking for him after class. I caught up with him, but before I could speak he said, "Hey, I was going to come find you to see what our homework was." I told him what the reading assignment was and he said he'd already done it. I then said that his rough draft was due in three days and asked if it would be ready since he had not turned in a concept paper. He said, "Well that's going to be a little tough since I don't have anything to write about." I was going to suggest he write about his academic struggles in school so I said, "Joe, think back to your freshman year when . . ."

"You mean Brian's accident?" he interrupted.

I smiled and blurted out "That's a great idea!" Truthfully, though it had been a bad accident, I'd almost forgotten about it.

"One of the things I could tell about," he continued, "is the day you and I brought him a Frosty."

"You sure could," I responded. "And I remember something you could use in your conclusion. The accident was in mid-November and the Tuesday before Thanksgiving my question of the day was, *what is one thing for which you are thankful? Do you* remember how you answered that question?"

"Yeah," he replied with a far-away smile. "I said, I'm thankful Brian didn't die."

When the class finished with the Buddha quote we did a little sharing. Some said that "do your best" meant try your hardest. Some said that only the individual person could know if they did their best. Katie wrote, "when I try to do my best, I feel good about myself."

I know I don't always do my best; I'm not sure anyone does. But I do know this: Somewhere out there is a former D average klutz who has done his best in the world of chemical engineering, in large part, probably, because Larry did *his* best. And I know that so far this year, Joe has earned a check-plus or a check-plus-plus on most of his reading quizzes, and the other day we

a

conferenced the rough draft of his personal narrative. Oh Katie, you are so right!

This column originally appeared in Foster's Daily Democrat, Dover, NH on September 29, 2009.

Is This My Land?

Any intelligent person who likes to read, and certainly any decent English or language arts teacher, will tell you that the real value of literature is found in how you can apply it to your life. Through his process of dying, Morrie Schwartz, with the help of author Mitch Albom in *Tuesdays with Morrie*, teaches us how to better live. Holocaust survivor, author, and professor Elie Wiesel, through his tragic experiences in *Night*, reminds us each time we read it of what must never be allowed to happen again. And I have never looked at my friendships nor considered potential friendships quite the same since the first time I read Chris Crutcher's *Staying Fat for Sarah Byrnes*, in which the protagonist risks everything so he can remain true to his best friend, whose face was severely burned and disfigured when she was a little girl.

Yes, there are many life issues I don't look at in quite the same way as a result of literature and how I apply it to my life. For example, a fairly common theme in some of the books, essays, and short stories we read in my classes is home ownership. I mean it's a big part of the American dream, right? It seems like most people want their little plot of land with a house. Some people want a big plot of land. Still others want many big plots of land.

One of the short stories my seniors study is Tolstoy's "How Much Land Does a Man Need." I often introduce the piece by asking each student, "How much land would you like to own someday?" Tolstoy presents for us an interesting drama of one man's quest for ever increasing amounts of land, tossing in elements of deceit, foul play, and outright greed along the way. It usually results in some interesting dialog and discussion in my classroom. How much land does someone really *need*? What is a responsible use of limited resources? What would "limits" mean in a capitalist system? Is capitalism really the best system, or is their something better?

In Steinbeck's *Of Mice and Men* Lennie and George, two farmhands who go from ranch to ranch during The Depression working for $50 a month, spend much of their free time dreaming of having their own place. They want just a few acres—a small farmhouse, enough land to plant a garden, raise a few animals, and "live off the fatta the lan." They don't want a lot, just a place to call their own.

Andre Dubus constructed his entire novel *House of Sand and Fog* around a house that had been in the protagonist's family for years but was lost as a result of a tax assessment error. Former President George W. Bush owns a ranch in Texas encompassing some sixteen hundred acres. That almost equals the land area of the entire town of Durham! And of course we can't forget Donald Trump, whose ongoing land acquisitions seem to suggest that no amount of land is *ever* enough.

There are others who might figure they've got enough, but what they want to do with it is the larger question. Supreme Court Justice David Souter took a lot of heat for a controversial vote concerning a Connecticut town that wanted to take by eminent domain some valuable waterfront land on which sat some run-down homes. The plan was to take the land and then sell it to a private developer who would tear down the existing houses. The real estate would then be redeveloped with more expensive buildings thus giving the town significantly greater property tax revenue.

A couple of years ago I was reminded, while enjoying the natural beauty of the University of New Hampshire's Browne Center ropes course, that if Aristotle Onasis had had his way back in the 1970s I'd have been standing in the middle of an oil refinery instead of group building with my students in a pristine wood nestled on the banks of the Great Bay estuary.

See, I have learned a few things over the years—some from literature, some from life experience, and some from friends. Several years ago I was at an informal gathering of friends, and somehow I got ranting and raving about a piece of land I owned. I don't even remember what piece. What I do remember is going off on this elderly preacher friend of mine—getting louder and more animated as I went: "You know I ought to be able to do what I want to with my own land. I bought it, I pay the taxes on it, I *own* it, darn it, it's *mine!*" I'm pretty sure the final clause was accompanied by a stomp of my right foot. Well, my preacher friend looked up at me from his sitting position and simply said in a very calm, loving voice somewhat crunchy with age, "No it isn't, Steve, you're just the steward of it."

I've thought about that exchange many times over the years, and I tell it in my classes every semester. Wars have been fought over land. Fortunes have been lost over land. People have been cheated out of it. Lennie and George never stopped dreaming about it. Tolstoy's Bashkirs were willing to sell it. Politicians bargain, manipulate, and accommodate with it. George Bush has it and Donald Trump is always looking for more of it. But you know what? My old preacher friend was right: he, they, or me, we're all just stewards of it. Thank goodness, too, because who knows what we might do with it if we really did "own" it. Besides, as my students discover each year when we read the Tolstoy piece, and we suffer through Pahom's fatal quest for more and more land, in the end we really only *need* six feet anyway.

This column originally appeared in Foster's Daily Democrat, Dover, NH on May 5, 2009.

Accountability

Accountability is one of the buzz words in education today. Local district school boards are trying to hold teachers accountable, the state boards of education are trying to hold districts accountable, and the federal government is trying to hold everyone accountable—except itself, of course. And they are all looking at essentially one thing: test scores. Oh, there may be some other factors tossed in, but test scores is what they really want to see.

Honestly, I don't think "accountability" is a dirty word, even as it pertains to teachers. I think we teachers should be held accountable; we should be held accountable by our students. Early in my undergrad work at the University of New Hampshire I was having to "update my high school transcripts." I didn't have enough college math in high school to satisfy my UNH academic advisor and so I found myself taking Math 302, the college equivalent of high school Algebra II, during the summer of 1993.

I remember my Math 302 instructor—I'll call him Mr. Smith. Mr. Smith had a wealth of experience having taught high school algebra for some thirty years, and he could get all sorts of algebraic information on the board fast—so fast you couldn't get the equations copied down before he was done with the solution and already moved on to the next problem.

I could tell right away he was one of those guys who would just get stuff, lots of stuff, onto the board. It was then up to us to actually learn it. Well, at thirty-six years old I wasn't easily intimidated—not even by academicians. I guess I sort of had this belief that I, specifically my tuition, was part of the reason he had a job. So, at maybe the second class session, just before he was

71

about to erase his board full of formulas, equations, and solutions, I raised my hand and said, "Excuse me. I am not brilliant, nor am I a dunce. Make it make sense to me." And guess what? He did.

That's the kind of accountability I'm talking about. I *want* to be held accountable—by my students, not by some politician or bureaucrat. I want my students to demand the best that I have to offer. If I'm going to test or assess it in some way, they should make darn sure I've taught it, and taught it well. I want them asking questions. I want them making me defend my beliefs and positions and ideas and answers. They should hold me to the standards to which I hold them, in writing, in reading, in speaking, and in critical thinking. My job is to help them become more literate, so I want my students to make me make sense to them.

You see, literacy is more than mastering the many rhetorical strategies and literary devices, or learning proper capitalization and punctuation. It's more than boosting lexile and comprehension scores. It's more than any of those things, singularly or collectively—way more. In Dan Millman's *Way of the Peaceful Warrior* the character Dan, a world class gymnast, and his mentor Socrates have a conversation about what Dan will do with his life since college is nearing an end. Socrates suggests the possibility of teaching and Dan responds with, "I don't know what I'd teach besides gymnastics," to which Socrates replies, "Gymnastics is enough as long as you use it to convey more universal lessons." That's sort of how I feel about teaching English: English is enough as long as I use it to convey more universal lessons.

Chris Crutcher, author of *Staying Fat for Sarah Byrnes*, a novel about a horribly disfigured girl, mentions in a short essay a middle school student who'd written to him saying that, "though she wasn't a kid with Sarah Byrnes' life . . . she thought she might be one of those people who is mean to kids like Sarah. 'This story made me want to be a better person.'" That's a more universal lesson.

I had a freshman student this last semester who had a very hard time doing his homework. Yet he wrote a short narrative so he could speak at the memorial service of a favorite cousin. He then asked me if I though he could use the piece to deliver to our class as part of his final exam. That's a more universal lesson.

A few days ago I ran into Ryan and Stephanie along with several members of their family at a local restaurant. Ryan and Stephanie had been in my very first senior honors English class back in 1998. They had married after college and still live in the area. As my group was leaving the restaurant Ryan's mom followed me out. She wanted to tell me how much of an impact I had made on both Ryan and Stephanie. She said she was certain that I was a big part of the reason Ryan had gone into teaching and become such a good teacher. Then she said, "And I still remember Stephanie saying at the end of your course, 'you know, he went around the room and said something special about every single person in the class.'" That's a more universal lesson.

I once had a student who was petrified to give her speech in front of the class—petrified. She stood at the podium and began to cry. She started her speech, still crying, and never completely stopped. But with the encouragement of the entire class she made it through her speech, tears and all, and gave me a hug afterwards. That's a more universal lesson.

Those, folks, for all the things that might be right with it, those are the things that government imposed "accountability" doesn't measure. Those are the standards to which I want to be held accountable—to which I *should* be held accountable.

This column originally appeared in Foster's Daily Democrat, Dover, NH on July 14, 2009.

PART III

THE GOOD, THE BAD, AND THE REALLY SAD

Like most teachers, I have had numerous experiences over the years with students, administrators, and colleagues, with school board members and parents. Most have been wonderful, exhilarating even. Some have been downright maddening, and a few heartbreaking—not unlike most people's professional lives, I suspect.

There were the times like the day our superintendent came to tell us all that we had been pink-slipped due to a budget battle. Not, mind you, that some faculty, or even a lot of faculty, but all faculty had been pink-slipped. It was nothing more than grandstanding in a pissing match with the city council over the budget. Rather than spend the necessary time negotiating, strategizing, and prioritizing they took the easy way out—the nuclear option you might say—to whip up public sentiment. Think about what happened to many people's vacation plans, pending mortgage applications, etc. All because the school board couldn't or wouldn't do their job!

I recall being asked to attend a "parent" meeting one time concerning a student with whom I'd had a run-in over a hat I had asked him to remove—a request he totally ignored, though the hat violated school policy. So upon entering the office, I sat down with the student, a woman with a baby carriage, whom I assumed was his mother or stepmother, and my principal. At one point I remember saying something to which the student took offense and he said, "Hey, you can't talk to my father's girlfriend like that." My eyes went from the student to my principal. I never uttered a word of response, but my look said, "Really? This is what we've come to? I have to sit here and defend myself, or at least justify myself, to some kid's father's *girlfriend*?" Oh yes, there have been some bad times. But honestly they were very few and very, very far between.

I cannot tell you the number of emails, cards, and notes I have received over the years thanking me for a phone call to a parent thanking *them* for sharing their child with me; or for highlighting their student in my graduation speech, or going to their home to help their sick or suspended child make up a test; or the accolades and applause I received from the middle school chorus director for accompanying their Christmas concert—with about twenty-four hours notice.

I can't tell you how many times I have been moved to tears from students saying things like, "I would never have made it through high school if it weren't for you," or, "Mr. MacKenzie, I can't thank you enough for helping me be a better writer and reader, but most of all for helping me be a better person." There was one time I called home and got a student's dad. I greeted him and said I had just called to tell him how much I was enjoying getting to know his son, that he was a fun guy, usually prepared for class, always respectful, and generally a pleasure to have in class, and I just wanted him to know that. There was a moment of silence and then he began to laugh and said, "Okay, Mr. MacKenzie, I appreciate your efforts, now go ahead and tell me why you really called." I'm not sure he ever completely believed me, but I think I finally convinced him! And then there was the time a young lady wrote in my year book thanking me for helping her get through her, *first ever*, in-class oral presentation—as a senior. She was on the verge (almost over it) of hyperventilation and tears for the entire thing, but she got through it! Those weren't good times, they were great times.

Then there were those few times that felt like they would kill me. The student who collapsed into my arms one morning instead of beginning our standard two-minute, ten or twelve element handshake, for he had just found out his cousin had died. The student who was hugging me after graduation, sobbing—body shaking sobbing—saying, "What am I going to do now Mr. MacKenzie, what am I ever going to do now?" You see, for that student, school was the safe place, the place where he felt valued, cared for, loved. And I was certain my heart would break attending the memorial services for Kendra, and Adam, and Alex, and James, and too many others. Those times were so incredibly ... sad.

Who the Heck
is Haim Ginott

Discipline is the bane of every teacher's existence in the classroom. Seasoned teachers have learned how to discipline, less experienced teachers hate to discipline, and brand new teachers won't have to discipline (after all, younger teachers are cooler and can relate to kids better and just will not have the problems the older folks do!). I have been all of the above. I have been the idealist, the new teacher with all the better ideas. I have been the *newer* teacher who had to confront the fact that every kid will not worship at his throne and that sometimes discipline is necessary. And I have been the experienced teacher who has still needed to learn a few things along the way.

One of the things I learned fairly early on was to employ at least some of the ideas of the late Haim Ginott. Haim Ginott was a twentieth-century Israeli teacher who, according to Ursula Morton, gained public attention in the 1960s for his views on education. Morton wrote that "one of his rather startling observations was children are our enemies and we don't know it, and we are their friends and they don't know it." Well, I am my students' friend and they know it. I'm not their buddy and I don't want to be. I am, however, their friend. But listen, even that does not guarantee a problem-free classroom.

So what do I do when I have a discipline problem? Nowadays, I look at my behavior at least as much as theirs, and I try to respond like a good teacher rather than like a frustrated student. I go to the sign tacked up on the bulletin board right behind where I sit and start reading as follows:

78

Stephen MacKenzie

ON TEACHING

I've come to a frightening conclusion that I am the
decisive element in the classroom.

It's my personal approach that creates the climate.

It's my daily mood that makes the weather.

As a teacher, I possess a tremendous power to make a
child's life miserable or joyous. I can be a tool of
torture or an instrument of inspiration. I can
humiliate or humor, hurt or heal.

In all situations, it is my response that decides
whether a crisis will be escalated or de-escalated,
and a child humanized or de-humanized.

--Haim Ginott

I will go to the sign on that board, face it with my hands folded
behind my back, read every word, turn back to the class, take my
seat, slowly exhale, and say, "Okay, I'm better now; let's
continue." It wasn't always that way, though.

A couple of years ago I had a class of freshmen that made me
crazy. They would laugh, yell, joke, and cuss—anything but work.
No matter what I tried it wasn't enough. I couldn't be creative
enough, or engaging enough. I failed at motivation: Positive
reinforcement, negative reinforcement, outright bribery. In the
end I still tossed more kids out of that class in one semester than
in all my other eight year's worth of classes combined. Oh yeah, I
had all the discipline answers! You have no idea how many times

I had listened to colleagues bemoaning an unpleasant situation with one or more students. Then I would sort of semi-smugly reply, "Gee, I rarely have discipline problems in my room." I'll bet some of those colleagues wanted to smack me. Let me just say this, during those freshmen days—boy did I get mine! And to make matters worse I spent too little time reading my sign and too much time reacting to bad behavior. Oh I had the "power" alright and I used it, but not always to de-escalate and humanize—too often it was simply to demonstrate my possession of it.

Yes, with that group of freshmen I played the power card all right, and knew I would win. But they raised the ante, called my hand, and knew they would win—and they were right. I made phone calls home, scheduled parent/teacher meetings, handed out detentions, and threw students out of class. I was miserable— they were having a blast. Finally I decided to really listen to Ginott's words rather than just read them. I started trying to conjure up some sunshine and warm temperatures. I tried to inspire rather than punish, humanize instead of humiliate—to really *be* the friend I professed to be.

Something must have finally gotten through somehow, because almost all of them passed and several of those I was tossing out the most have been among the ones who are most eager to greet me when I get back from my second semester vacation each year. Did it have anything to do with visits to the hospital and Wendy's Frosties after Joe's cousin was in a car accident? Was it because I went to Gina's house to give her a test when she'd been suspended? Can I point to all the hours I gave a bunch of them after school helping out with make-up work? Or how about the genuine sadness I shared with Frankie when he came to tell me he was moving? Maybe it was some of those things, maybe it was all of those things, but I think it had a lot more to do with *showing* the respect and tolerance I expected of them; a retooling for inspiration, humor, and healing. Even that wasn't really it, though. It was their acquired knowledge that after all the threatening, punishing, and tossing I was still going to be their friend, whether they wanted me or not.

Haim Ginott died a half a century ago—but thank goodness he left some of his wisdom here. "Mr. Mac," I heard behind me one day, "what are you reading?" "The weather report," I replied as I sat back down, exhaling slowly, "and it's clearing, so let's continue."

This column originally appeared in Foster's Daily Democrat, Dover, NH on August 16, 2007.

When Will I Ever Use This?

Do you want to annoy your teacher, assuming you're a student of course? I mean *really* annoy your teacher. Ask the one question all teachers hate to hear, especially math teachers, and be sure to add just a bit of whine to it: *When will I ever use this?*

Think about it; how stupid is that question? Yeah, I know, the only stupid question . . . blah, blah, blah. No, some questions *are* stupid, and usually that is one of them. I don't know when you may need to use a standard five-paragraph essay. I don't know when you might need to write a piece of poetry, understand the concept of velocity, work with fractions or use algebraic equations, use the formula for burning calories and fat, remember something about the Vietnam War, or know the definition of some Latin phrase. I am not a soothsayer, I have no crystal ball, and I have no idea what you will end up doing for a living.

In my case I teach English. English teachers need to know that the *subject* does the verb and the *object* receives the action of the verb, so we don't say things like "Me and her are going to the store." We need to know the difference between active and passive voice so we don't sound like those idiots on the TV court shows with their "Your Honor, if I would have just known that she had went I would not have went myself," or "we figured it out when me and him was *conversating*." We need to know that a lead paragraph is immediately engaging, the body of the text is fully developed with concrete details, and that a good conclusion refers back to the major points of the paper so we provide a successful closure rather than just an ending.

But even English teachers don't always know when they're

going to use everything they've had to learn. My colleagues and I decided to spend some time this summer working with standardized test data from the past year to help us revise our curriculum and instruction, hopefully better meeting student needs (academic jargon for *boost their scores!*). We discovered, for one thing, we were not doing enough with basic English grammar—things like capitalization and punctuation, subject verb agreement, prefixes and suffixes and vocabulary. What we realized was that we were leaving too much of that kind of instruction to the lower grades and spending more of our time on reading, critical thinking, literature, and more advanced writing.

Well, that discovery led to an interesting discussion about SAT prep, as well as our honors English courses and the AP English exam. And that led to a query about the definition of *synecdoche* (using a smaller piece to represent a whole, i.e. *would you give me a hand with this?*) and the difference between *synecdoche* and *metonymy* (the substitution of a related word for the word itself, i.e. *I need a Kleenex please*). At some point we learned these terms but at the beginning of the conversation we couldn't even come up with accurate pronunciations (synecdoche = sin-EK-duh-key; metonymy = mĕ-TAWN-ĕ-mēē). How did we know when we'd ever use that information? We didn't and we may never use it again, but we did that day.

Now I don't know how math, science, or history teachers respond to the *"when will I ever use this"* question, but I know how I do: "probably never!—unless of course you want to be perceived as a literate human being who can read a newspaper or magazine, write a thank-you note, draft a cover letter for an application packet, or carry on an intelligent conversation employing something beyond one-syllable, four-letter words. In other words, folks, you'll use these things every day of your lives should you choose to become successful, contributing members of society."

I know some other things, too. If you master the five-paragraph essay as a freshman, you'll have a heck-of-a-lot easier time with the five to seven *page* papers you'll get as a senior. You may even discover you can use some of your math skills in English. For instance, we were reading Dan Millman's *Way of the Peaceful Warrior* last year when we came across this equation:

$$Happiness = \frac{Satisfaction}{Desires}$$

We had quite the conversation about that one. We even tried plugging in some numbers to represent the words. Remember this is an equation not just a fraction. One of the things we discovered was you are always going to have some desires because the denominator can't be zero. Of course that makes a lot more sense if you can define the term *denominator*!

I know that figuring out how much grass seed I need when I build a new house is a simple matter if I know some basic math formulas and concepts. I know my wife loves it when I write her little notes, and I remember one Christmas when we were pretty strapped financially that I wrote and framed a poem about and for each of my stepchildren—they cherished them! I know that I am a healthier person because I've learned something about the food groups, nutrition, and burning calories from my science classes. I know you might not want to wait until you're reconstructing an accident to learn about the principles of velocity—because it may be too late. I hope it's not in a plea bargain session that you first encounter *quid pro quo*, and I hear a whole lot of US Senators every day talking about Vietnam and repeating history. Bet they wish they'd spent more time studying the Gulf of Tonkin Resolution.

"So what if I don't care about being a brain—what about me and what I need to learn?" someone could still ask. Hey, Judge Judy's on at 4:00; I suggest you listen in.

This column originally appeared in Foster's Daily Democrat, Dover, NH on August 2, 2007.

The Class from Hades

As much as I would like to I can't let you think that I just have a giant love-fest in my classroom every day. I mean I do have my moments—and every once in a great while, the first one being my first year, I even have my . . . class from Hades. We all know where I really mean but I don't use foul language in my classroom and I'm not going to use it in the newspaper either, even if it's allowed.

That is not to say there weren't some great kids in the class, for there were, but man, it was a tough mix of kids from the beginning. To start with, that was the class with Jolene. She was the one who, on the first day of school, accosted me with, *Are you a real teacher?* Yup, that was her first question on the first day!

Then there was Andy, the first student to tell me to go F myself (though he used the entire word). "I don't think so," I said, "take a walk to the office." There was Nick, who hollered across the room one day to a *friend*, "You can get your own F'ing ride home." I had to throw him out as well. And I can't forget Josh. Josh leaned back in his chair one day near the end of the first quarter and virtually belched out, "Jeeesuuuus Chriiiiist, the same old s--- every day. They told us that with block scheduling we'd get a lot more variety of stuff, not the same old s--- every day." I glared at him in amazement for a second and spit back, "They lied!" I began to wonder if he was the one who'd lifted my rank book a couple of days earlier. I had returned to my classroom one day from lunch to discover it had been stolen. I don't remember my threat but it reappeared the next day— apparently intact.

Now let me tell you about Rachel, whose vocabulary consisted of little beyond the family of four-letter words and their immediate relations. She wouldn't answer questions, refused to read aloud, and generally specialized in being a pain. It got so bad that I finally insisted on a meeting with her parents, but quickly realized they would be little help. Her father asked me how I thought I could disallow foul language in my classroom when we were working with Tim O'Brien's *The Things They Carried.* "Are you suggesting that high school students can't differentiate between foul language in the context of literature and foul language in conversation? For if you are, sir, I can assure you that you are wrong. Yes, I think my students can make that distinction—your daughter can make that distinction, she chooses not to." I went on to say that his daughter used language in my classroom that I suspected would even embarrass him. His response was, "Well, I'm sure that's probably true, Mr. MacKenzie, but I sort of see that as a sign of our times, don't you?" "Yes, I do, sir, because many of us allow it—I won't."

Even some of the good kids, who never swore or fought in class, bummed me out at times. Like I had this guy Doug. He was respectful, never talked back, was almost always prepared, and got some of the best grades in the class. We were chatting during break one day and he mentioned how much he disliked what we were doing. With a great deal of surprise I said, "But I thought you did like it—you're so *good* at it." He replied, "No, I'm not." I insisted, "Doug, you are." He replied, "No, I'm really not, I'm just a good student." I was at a loss for words, so I guess he was right.

At least one other time I was at a loss for words and that was with dear Jolene. Jolene did little beyond shoot her mouth off and be generally disruptive in class. She would read, occasionally, but did little other classroom work and never did homework. I tried to convince her to take our work more seriously, that poor grades would impact her college chances, her eligibility to play sports. It made no difference. By the time I was calculating first quarter report-card grades I was sure Jolene would be one of my casualties. Imagine my surprise to discover she was passing, and not even with a D but with a C! I looked at the calculator again, thinking *her grade can't possibly be that high.* So I went back through to see if I had divided by the wrong number of assignments—I had not. I went back through each column to see if I had added wrong—I had not. I then went back through each individual assignment and its grade—slowly—to see where I had erred. Then I saw it. *There is no way she got a 90 on that test—no way,* I thought. Then I remembered my missing rank book and knew it was not Josh who had taken it. Looking carefully I could tell that the grade had been changed—from a 60 to a 90. She had erased the 60 and written in a 90, the faint erased grade was still just barely visible. So what do I do now, I lamented. I mean what could I do—call her a liar? I was so ticked off and frustrated—by her arrogance, by my stupidity, and by a lack of any hard evidence with which to accuse her. What the heck could I do? Then it came to me. I got out a pencil, erased the 90, and wrote the 60 back. I mean what could she do—call me a liar?

This column originally appeared in Foster's Daily Democrat, Dover, NH on May 10, 2007.

Throwing Our Arms Up

I've come to a certain understanding about teaching—sometimes I do the teaching, sometimes my students do the teaching, and sometimes we just sort of throw up our arms and quit—for the moment. I'm okay with that. They know more about kid culture, who and what's hot, snapchat, tweets, and smartphones than I do. I know more about literature, diction, syntax, etymology, and epistemology than they do. Then there are those things that neither they nor I know enough about, *how did the world begin? why do bad things happen to good people? is there life after death?* where we may just throw up our arms and admit defeat—sometimes.

In September of 2004 I lost a student. His name was Adam and we had been pretty close since his freshman year. In the days that followed his tragic car accident, wake, and memorial service my students and I were pretty defeated. Now make no mistake, Adam was not a teacher's dream scholar. He was highly unmotivated when it came to work—particularly homework. I don't know how many calls I made to his cell phone to remind him that something was due, probably overdue. He was a terrible procrastinator and almost never stopped talking. And one of the few days he didn't talk too much in class was the day he was keeping score on the number of times I had to say, "please be quiet," or "please stop talking." I think the count was something like thirty-six times. So no, Adam was not a teacher's dream scholar, but he was a teacher's dream student. This I know, because he was one of my dream students. Adam trusted me and always acted respectful, even when I was having to chew him out. He was never unkind in my classroom. He never played the victim, never looked for someone else to blame, and I don't believe he ever told me a lie, even when the truth was painful. He wasn't a perfect kid, just a great one, and one of mine.

Because we had been so close, and because I had spoken at his graduation, Adam's mom asked me if I would speak at his memorial service. "Of course," I responded, wondering how I could ever manage to control my own grief enough to help others deal with theirs. In my eulogy I remember confessing, "Folks, there is nothing I can say, no joke I can tell, no cliché I can retell, not even any original prose I can compose that will take away the pain we are all feeling. I wish there were, for I'd tell it or retell it or write it." I'm still not exactly sure how, but we did make it through the service and the day—barely.

The thing that amazed me was that it didn't go away, the incredible grief I mean. The days and weeks that followed his memorial service were as painful as the day following the accident. We talked about it in my classes where I still had a number of his closest friends. They had questions that needed answers, answers from me, and my knowledge of etymology or my skills in composition were not going to provide them. I talked to several colleagues and friends seeking their advice about how to help my kids through this tragedy. I thought back to some of the literature we had studied in class, the novels, essays, even the Bible parables from their senior anthology, and tried to find some answers in them, along with some relief.

So for several days following the accident I looked for ways in which I could "help" through our class work. We started with some of the losses Dan Millman dealt with in *Way of the Peaceful Warrior*, yet a shattered leg didn't quite measure up to a shattered life. I assigned a journal write but their responses left more questions than answers. In the end what I came to realize was that *I* needed at least as much help as they did, and at the suggestion of a friend I tried one of the things I do best; fighting back tears I told the kids a story:

A long time ago there was this guy named Moses who was the leader of a group of people called the Isrealites. Now the Isrealites tended to whine a lot when things didn't go their way but basically they were good people. Well the Isrealites were attacked one day by a tribe called the Amalekites. Moses ordered one of his best leaders to take their soldiers into battle to defend against these Amalekites. He then took two of his closest friends to the top of a nearby hill to watch the armies as they fought.

As long as Moses stood with his arms outstretched the Isrealites maintained the edge in the battle. But you know you can only keep your arms stretched out for so long before your muscles get tired and you have to drop your arms to rest. And as soon as Moses had to drop his arms the Amalekites would gain the upper hand. Once Moses had rested and was able to extend his arms again the Isrealites would retake the superior position.

Eventually the two friends noticed what was happening. So one stepped to the left of Moses and the other to the right. Each time Moses became tired the men would simply hold up his arms. That way Moses was able to keep his arms up for as long as it took the Isrealites to win.

Beginning to lose the tear battle by the time I finished, I said to the class, "I know somehow I can be strong enough to get through Adam's death, and I can be strong enough to help you all get through it, too—but sometimes . . . I may need you to help hold my arms up.

This column originally appeared in Foster's Daily Democrat, Dover, NH on January 18, 2007.

A Disappointed Family

I have a new sign hanging in my room this year: *WE ARE FAMILY*. Technically I stole it from TNT's The Ron Clark Story, but I actually got the idea from something a former student wrote in his end-of-course letter: "This class has changed me significantly in one way. It was a small class and we all sat in a tight area, and it helped us become close. I never thought I would think of my fellow classmates as some sort of family, but I do now. Each of us is unique, which added to the whole family atmosphere. At times it didn't even feel like we were in Honors English IV but more like at a family dinner. And I know that sometimes we pissed you off and sometimes we could irritate each other, but isn't that what happens in most families?"

Last Saturday was a hard day to be in the athletic family at Somersworth High, and Monday was a hard day to be a teacher of those athletes. At one o'clock that Saturday our No.1 seeded Hilltoppers football team took on the No. 4 St. Thomas Saints in the division semi-finals—a game we were confident we would win. After all, the Saints only made it into the playoffs because we won our last regular season game. And then at five o'clock our No. 2 seeded girls volleyball team took on undefeated Gilford for their division championship, a game we had no real thought of winning. The boys fought through until the last two minutes of the game and the girls took their match to a fifth game, something that had happened to Gilford only once during the entire season. Yes, in both cases the wins came down to the last few minutes of the game, and they were not ours.

So what does an English teacher do on a day like the following

Monday, particularly when he has twelve of those athletes in two of his classes? We do a writing exercise. The prompt I gave was this:

> All of us from time to time will suffer disappointment. Sometimes it will be mild, other times bitter. In *Way of the Peaceful Warrior* Dan Millman claimed that "there are no accidents . . . only lessons." Applying that idea, in a well-developed response, describe a time you suffered disappointment.

Not surprisingly, the responses were weighted toward the weekend's losses. And the losses weighed heavily. They talked about how "disappointed [they] were," about how "it wasn't supposed to be this way," and "the title that I thought was already ours was gone forever." They wrote about how hard they had worked and practiced for the entire season, their "Cinderella Season" as Brett said—only to come up with a loss. What I felt really good about, though, was that they also wrote about other things. Abby talked about the "great bunch of girls" she played with and that "[she is] going to miss them very much next year and many years after that." Dave said that while he learned "you can't always expect things to go your way . . . the bigger lesson is friendship and teamwork. Friendship should be valued more than anything . . . because it gives reason and purpose for your life." Twan put it this way: "I am still the same as before, still with the same friends that I will continue to laugh with and have fun with. We lost a game but we didn't lose each other."

Truly, they rarely cease to amaze me. Meg wrote that "losing the championship was a disappointment, but I am not ashamed of it. We played very well against Gilford, better than we have ever played against them, and in games one and three, probably the best we have ever played! We made it to the championship. To me that is a great accomplishment. Out of the many teams that wanted to be there it was us." And Chris told us that for him, as bitter as the loss was, the end of the season, the end of the team was the bigger loss, "the greatest loss I have ever had." German exchange student Jan K. had similar feelings, writing that "usually disappointment ends in a form of hate . . . We tried to make it go away, yes . . . with love."

And I admit there were a couple that really got to me. Drew wrote, "The biggest game in my nine-year football career . . . We were the team to beat; the number one seed going into the playoffs versus the number four seed, and we lost . . . I will never again play ball under the lights on our home field with all of my buddies that I grew up with—*ever* again . . . I just wanted to be a champion my senior year."

Then there was Bryant who wrote that "It first hit me when I solemnly walked off the field after throwing my last pass, a ball intended for Chris. I realized that moment I'd never take another snap for the 'Toppers . . . After all the tears and hugs with my teammates I walked out onto the field by myself. I looked from end zone to end zone and thought about all the years on this field . . . . Luke walked over to me and patted me on the shoulder, 'There was nobody better to look up to than you Bryant.'"

Bryant, *that* is the lesson: what it's all about. I don't care if you leave my class and our school and never win another game. But I care deeply that you are someone people can look up to. Meg, it *was* a great accomplishment. Drew, you *are* a champion, and it doesn't have a thing to do with that game. And to all of the rest of you—I am so proud you are part of my family.

This column originally appeared in Foster's Daily Democrat, Dover, NH on November 9, 2006.

* Note: Sadly, Bryant passed away in 2016. Bodies die but love lives on. Rest in peace, my friend, for I love you still.

— Mr. Mac

Dealing with Disappointment

Following some significant play-off losses a few months ago, I had my students write responses to a prompt that dealt with disappointments. The majority of them wrote about sports losses; not all of them were the fall volleyball championship or football semi-finals, but sports losses nonetheless. One of them, however, did not. One of them, written by Alan, a senior honors student, reached out and grabbed me. Perhaps it will grab you as well. He wrote:

"One of the most disappointing times in my life was not the loss of a sports game. It wasn't failing a test or failing a class. It was when one of my best friends since first grade dropped out of high school. It didn't make a lot of sense to me. Throughout the years he had always done better than me. Yet, I've made it and he hasn't . . . knowing that in only about seven months I'll be graduating and he won't be is a huge disappointment.

It's pretty disappointing to say I barely know a person I've been close friends with since I was six. Sometimes I wonder why it was him instead of me. None of it makes any sense at all. It's hard to believe he left two years ago. I remember finding out in Mrs. Blanner's class. It left me blank. I'm disappointed [he] isn't here today. I'm disappointed that he won't be here in June. I'm disappointed that he gave up so fast. Most of all I'm disappointed because he didn't give me the chance to try and stop him. It's been two years and I don't see the disappointment ending anytime soon."

Maybe Alan's response grabbed me because I felt the tears

welling as he shared it in class—and then welling again as I read it myself later that evening. Maybe it grabbed me because I've dedicated my entire staff development plan for the current cycle to working on reducing our dropout rate. Maybe it's because I can scarcely stand to see one of my students in pain. But, probably it's because I firmly believe that in some way we have failed a student who decides to drop out of high school, at least we're part of it, for I also firmly believe in a slogan I picked up one year at a Teacher's Convention workshop: It's our job to run schools that kids want to come to.

Two years ago I helped organize and facilitate a group whose sole function was to look for new ways to reduce our staggering dropout rate. We held a dialogue forum with some former students who had dropped out. We kicked off a mentor program linking struggling students with an adult mentor. We became more proactive in trying to engage potential dropouts. Last year the district instituted a very clear attendance policy. This year, through a federal grant, we have become a Positive Behavioral Interventions and Supports (PBIS) school, following in the steps of our Somersworth elementary and middle schools. PBIS is designed to help reduce dropout rates by reducing the number of administrative referrals students receive due to behavior issues. The result of all of these efforts has been a rather dramatic decrease in the number of students dropping out of Somersworth High School.

So, we've substantially increased the daily attendance rate, and substantially decreased the dropout rate. Seems like we should be happy, right? Then why was I talking to a student recently who said to me, "Mr. MacKenzie, all I want to do is stay out of trouble and out of the assistant principal's way for the next six months until I turn sixteen so I can dropout"?

Why do we have students who come to school every day with

nothing and do nothing? Why do we have students who would rather face a suspension, or even an expulsion hearing, than attend classes and do some work? Why do so many US students see school as an aggravation and a useless waste of time, while kids from other countries see school as a gift and an opportunity? It seems pretty clear to me that it is not party time yet.

We may be running a school that some kids want to come to, or a lot of kids, maybe even most kids, but we obviously aren't running a school that all kids want to come to. No, I'm not going to beat myself up, but I'm not going to celebrate yet, either. I want kids to choose going to classes over hiding out in stairwells. I want them to choose education over expulsion. And if we have to offer young adult authors like Chris Crutcher over Steinbeck, Hemmingway, or Hawthorne to get kids to read, so be it. If we have to pull writing prompts from People Magazine instead of the Riverside Reader, it's not the end of the world.

I hated Huxley and his "new world," and I can't see forcing it on students if they'd rather read something else. I want them connected to school, whether it's through football, hockey, Interact, the drama club, Student Council, Gay Straight Alliance, or the Bible Club. I want them to feel valued and respected, in black fishnet stockings and a Mohawk, in dress shirts and khakis, or girlie jeans and a mullet. I want fewer behavioral problems and even less truancy. I want fewer students to fail courses. Mostly, I want the greatest disappointment of my student's high school experience to be the sadness of a lost ball game, not the tragedy of a lost friend.

This column originally appeared in Foster's Daily Democrat, Dover, NH on February 8, 2007.

Writing about Reading

I started something new in my English I class this year: independent reading. Every student has to have something outside the scope of the curriculum to read. I can't give a lot of class time for independent reading but I can give some. My goal is for my students to read for 15-20 minutes three times a week. I don't always make it but most weeks I do. And within some pretty broad but obvious limits, I don't really care what it is they bring to read. They can bring Stephen King or *People* magazine. They can bring novels or short stories. They can bring classic or contemporary poetry. They can bring fiction, nonfiction, comic books, essays, anthologies, anything—except our class textbook. I do feel strongly that it needs to be something that is not directly related to school.

So why, one might ask, heck *I* might ask if it was my kid's class, am I taking valuable instructional time for something that students can just as easily do at home? Easy—because they don't, at least in too many cases they don't. Do you have any idea how many of my students claim to be lousy or struggling writers? Do you know how many of them have little to no idea about many, maybe even most, of the major issues confronting our nation and world? Some don't have a strong vocabulary. Others have weak composition skills. And too many aren't conversant about much beyond Fire Emblem, Madden, and ipods. Their verbal skills don't go much further than "Hey, like, do you want to, like, hang out tonight?" Their writing abilities are compromised by their superior "what r u 2 doing" texting abilities, and their reading skills, well the newspaper industry is not going into the toilet because young people are reading too much. They don't know a complex sentence from a run-on, or a complete sentence from a fragment.

The greatest contributing factor to all these academic struggles, for kids and adults alike, is people don't read enough. Parents don't have or don't take enough time to read to their children. Children don't learn to enjoy reading for themselves. Consequently, too many adults would rather watch somebody else's imagination on a video screen than let their own imagination run wild through a good book. I actually had a student last week write his persuasive paper on reading. Craig's thesis, prominent in his lead paragraph, was that "everybody should *invest* (my italics) a minimum of thirty minutes a day in a good book, newspaper, or magazine." I thought I had died and gone to Heaven. I couldn't wait to find out what had hooked this eighteen-year-old-muscular-football-playing-high-school-male on reading, and I discovered that

"As a young lad I, like many, discovered the Harry Potter series by J.K. Rowling. Video games and television went on hold when it came to Harry's adventures. I read the books over and over again for two whole years. Entrenching myself deeply into the plot, the strength of my focus affected my mood and energy level of the present. When Rowling made a joke I laughed out loud. If a main character died I felt emotional pain."

Talk about getting into a book! But my excitement didn't stop there. Craig went on.

"And then Hollywood produced 'Harry Potter and the Sorcerer's Stone,' starring Daniel Radcliffe as Harry. Excited to get a new buzz from my favorite story I entered the theater with expectations stretched beyond reasonable limits. Within the first minute of viewing, distractions were pouring down on me with hurricane force. The director had completely misinterpreted the neighborhood design, McGonagal's voice abused my ears, and Harry didn't look like Harry! I left the theater that night wishing I'd stayed home. I choose the motion pictures of my imagination over anything DreamWorks has to offer."

And still the sway of the paper went on as he made other equally valuable points regarding the power of reading.

"Reading books and novels during your thirty minutes is not all I am suggesting. Some people simply aren't hooked by the lures of fantasy and adventure . . . I'm talking politics, sports, technology, etc. The number of publications out there that are significant to you is staggering. Just try Googling the term "Gardening." I found 79,800,000 results in 0.10 seconds. Devote thirty minutes a day to reading about gardening and I can assure you that by next growing season you will be an expert with plants . . . Getting your nose into the news also makes you feel more intelligent. I tell you, after reading the paper on Sunday morning you could throw me in with any group of businessmen or politicians and I would absolutely have something worthwhile to say."

I have no doubt Craig is telling the truth. I have written columns about individual students. I have written about kids, parents, and other teachers. I've written about vocabulary, classroom games, comedies and tragedies. I've often written about writing. Today I'm writing about reading. You want your kids to be smarter? Get them to read. You want your school's test scores to go up? Get your students to read. Hey, all you kids out there! Reading will help you build your vocabulary. Reading will help you be a better speller. Reading will help you become more intelligent. It has worked for Craig and it will work for you. It doesn't matter if you read *Foster's Daily Democrat*, the *New York Times*, or *The National Inquirer*. I don't care if you read *Popular Mechanics*, *Newsweek*, or *Rolling Stone*. You can read Toni Morrison, or Robert Ludlum, or Dan Brown, or Danielle Steele—it doesn't matter. And even if you don't end up an expert gardener, reading more of anything will help you be a better reader and a better writer. Reading will help you be a better thinker. Reading will just help you be better.

This column originally appeared in Foster's Daily Democrat, Dover, NH on October 7, 2008.

Putting Kids First

A recent series of things have convinced me it's time to tread on dangerous ground again. First, I read Jason Claffey's article in the July 12th *Sunday Citizen* called "Jon & Kate they're not." Secondly, I just got done reading Caitlin Flanagan's "Why Marriage Matters" in the July 13th issue of *Time* magazine. And finally, I have had some feedback from a reader who said that one of the things he appreciates about my column and hopes I "never change it" is that I "write realistically about what it is like to be a teacher." Well folks, it's time to be "real" again, even if it means risking a few steps on that dangerous ground.

The thing I liked most about the featured family in the *Citizen* article, specifically the three adults, was not that there had been a divorce, certainly a sad event, but that following a divorce, and remarriage for one of the ex-spouses, all three worked like a restauranteur on opening day to put the needs of the kids first. They "are able to sit near each other in the stands" at their kids' sporting events. "They attend parent-teacher conferences together. They spend holidays together. When one of the children is sick or injured, they ride together to the hospital." The needs of the kids come first.

Listen, I confess to being an optimist, even an idealist, but I'm not stupid. I know divorce happens—in 1978 I married a divorcé. And I know that in all likelihood if there are children they are going to suffer. But I also know that there are ways to minimize that suffering, and the best way is for the adults involved to behave like adults. I have students who will occasionally talk about their divorced parents who hate each other, who can't stand to be in the same building as the other let alone the same room. I have never understood that, not being able to be in the same room as an ex-spouse, even if he or she is remarried. No offense, it's not about you any longer, it's about the kids you chose to make. It's about supporting them in every way possible. If that means attending their games or concerts, then you'll need to be in the gym or the auditorium together. If it means coming to parent conferences, then you might need to be in the same room together, even sitting at a table together. As one of my favorite TV judges often admonishes feuding ex-spouses who appear before her, "You're supposed to love your kids more than you hate each other."

When my stepdaughter Donna got married she had very little money, so the entire event was held at our house, which was then on Northwood Lake. Her father, Ralph, now a retired clergyman, performed the ceremony, I gave her away, and her mother and stepmother put together and hosted the reception. I remember overhearing some of Donna's friends saying to her, "Wow! Your mother and your stepmother are at the same house, and they actually speak to each other. How did that happen?" Never especially good at holding my tongue I said, "Because that's what Donna needed and that's how *adults* behave when they need to do things for their kids." Some twelve years later we were all together again, only the latest of many family gatherings. This time we were all standing around a hospital bed at Dartmouth Hitchcock Medical Center looking at Jeffrey, our thirteen-month-old grandson who had been diagnosed with a brain tumor. Ralph baptized him and we stood shoulder to shoulder and prayed—because that's what Jeffrey needed.

Believe me, none of us is any kind of super human. We have done and said things over the years which ticked off one or more of the four of us. Typically they were unintentional slights but they happened nonetheless. The point is, ultimately they were not important. The kids were important.

In her *Time* essay Flanagan reported that a study released last May by the Center for Disease Control and Prevention showed that "births to unmarried women have reached an astonishing 39.7%." She goes on to ask, "How much does this matter? More than words can say. There is no other single force causing as much measurable hardship and human misery in this country as the collapse of marriage . . . It hurts children." This hurt sometimes shows up in my classroom.

I had a student once who talked about little other than his parents' divorce and the difficulty he had in dealing with their new boyfriends and girlfriends. This kid was in trouble most of the time—with teachers, with principals, with police. I remember a question of the day that asked students to *share something about which you are jealous of a friend*. The answer from one student was, "I'm kind of jealous of my friends who grew up with their moms, because I didn't have that." Another time the question was, *tell us about one of the hardest things you ever had to do*. One student answered, "I had to tell my mom that my dad was cheating on her." My students don't share things like these easily. It's painful for them. But I know they are things that need to be voiced (or they wouldn't voice them—kids don't relish showing pain or weakness) and I know they are shared from their hearts.

Perceptions of John and Kate aside, divorce might someday be your only viable option. But you can still put the needs of your children first. You can love your kids more than you hate your ex-spouse. They deserve it. You may have to sit beside each other at a parent - teacher conference. You may need to celebrate a birthday together, share in a wedding together, or pray by a hospital bed together.

This column originally appeared in Foster's Daily Democrat, Dover, NH on July 28, 2009.

Ode to Dickens

Today, the 30th of January, was one of those bittersweet days you hate to love, or love to hate. See yesterday I finished saying good-by to the last of my first semester students following their final exams. It's not like we won't see each other any more but we won't see each other in class. There were kids with whom I spent an intense weekend in Washington, D.C. learning about death and life and history, and forming bonds that will last a lifetime. There were others I agonized with through their first ever eight to ten page research paper, or their difficulty in learning forgiveness. We learned from authors, about the gift of life from Dan Millman, about death and dying and war from Elie Wiesel and Tim O'Brien, about loving from Mitch Albom and Morrie Schwartz. Yet it was Charles Dickens who flashed through my mind while I held one student as he cried because of having to move away, another as she told me of her parents' imminent divorce, and countless others as we warmly parted company at my classroom door.

I have spent five months learning and laughing and crying and loving and becoming a family with some of the most incredible people. Kelsie, one of my seniors, who'd been a bit skeptical at the beginning of the course with the whole "We Are Family" theme of my classroom, based her final presentation on just that concept. Among other things, she presented and discussed three definitions for "family," which her research had revealed. The first was "a group of people related by blood, perhaps living in the same house." Our classroom certainly didn't fit that description. The second dealt with "a classification of plants or animals which share certain biological or genetic traits." We didn't fit that one either. At this point she was going back to thinking she'd been right in the first place. But then she found definition number three: "a group of people bound together by common interests and concerns that nurtures and supports each other." We really *are* a family. These are the people to whom I had to say good-by. Can you imagine the grief we were all feeling?

Then came today, my first day of the new semester, first day without my old students, first day with a new prep period, a new lunch period, new kids, a new curriculum, new books, and new lesson plans. There was nothing familiar. Nobody came early to class so they could jam with me, or play Cribbage, or debate global warming. Block one came and my room was empty for the first time all year. If I'd had time it would have been depressing.

Fortunately, I didn't have time and my new prep, block one, flew by and all of a sudden it was block two and I was teaching English II for the first time in almost ten years. Then it was block three and I'm greeting second semester freshmen for the first time in my entire teaching career (I've had first semester freshmen but never second). So I immediately put them to work doing something I've never done before on the first day of class—I gave them a writing prompt for journaling. Now I often do in-class writing assignments right along with my kids, and I did this one. I'd like to share it with you:

I have to tell you that I am really going to miss my first semester classes. I had some awesome students and we did some great things together. I watched three different classes of students learn to live with each other, learn to support each other, learn to value and respect each other, learn to—in a very real way—become a family. Some of them will tell you they became better readers. Some of them will tell you they became better writers. Some of them will tell you they became better listeners. Some of them might even admit they'd become better lovers (of their friends and family). Many of them will tell you that in some way they became better people. They were people I grew to appreciate and value and love, and I will miss them.

That having been said, you have no idea how much I am looking forward to this new semester and my three knew classes—just from looking around the room. It's the one thing that takes the curse off losing my old ones. I've not taught English II in years, and I've never taught second semester freshmen before. I'm especially excited that some of you, by your own admission, are excited to be here. I can hardly wait to see what we accomplish together.

You know, when I got done writing that I truly was looking forward with much anticipation, so much so I was almost feeling a little guilty or disloyal. But it's all good, it really is all good. Where else could I "work" and help people prepare for medical careers, and law offices, and boardrooms, and child care, and business, and sales, and movies, and military service, and . . . where else could I do that? Dickens was right. Whether we're learning from famous authors through their works of literature or from each other as we walk the National Mall or assess each other's final presentations, whether we're laughing or crying, arguing or hugging, writing or reading, whether we're defining or redefining "family," whether we're packing up to move out or move in, in some ways they are the *best of times*, in other ways the *worst of times*. But they're always good times.

This column originally appeared in Foster's Daily Democrat, Dover, NH on February 3, 2009.

My Greatest Success

We were beginning our last full meeting of the year. The entire faculty and staff gathered in the conference room where the chairs were placed in a circle—of sorts. Even though it's a fairly large room, with some sixty-plus people present it was a tight fit.

Our assistant principal, Dana Hilliard, started the meeting off by sharing what he saw as his greatest success story of the year. He spoke of a student man who in September had been likely headed to jail or the Youth Detention Center in Manchester. With the help of a family who offered to assume legal guardianship, the administration, primarily Dana, was able to help broker a deal among the courts, SAU 56, and the police department which allowed this student to remain in Somersworth and stay in school. Choking back tears Dana said, "Last Wednesday that success walked across our lawn to receive a diploma. It had way more to do with other people than with me, but I still see it as my greatest success of the year."

Turning to his right we were then invited to share our success stories of the year. Nick, new to the building, talked about how warmly he'd been received. Several people talked about successes through PBIS. Gail talked about one of her students who had spent a lot of time dissing his intelligence, and then the pride she felt as she typed an "A" into her grading program: his final grade in oceanography.

I began to think, between speakers, about what I would share: maybe my seniors' field trip to Washington, D.C. or Luke inviting me to the top ten breakfast with him.

Coach Hogdson drew me back talking about the group of

athletes he'd just taken to Nationals in North Carolina. One of his students placed fourth for the high jump—in the entire nation—from little ol' Somersworth New Hampshire! Jimmy talked about the recycling program his students had begun and the new Environmental Club he started this year. Joan spoke about an office assistant she had this year and how much she had come to appreciate this person—after a very trying start.

Maybe I'll talk about the sympathy card my sophomores sent to Heather when her grandmother died or the notes a couple of my freshmen left on my desk, each of which said, "just wanted to say I love you and have a great summer."

Snapping back I heard Pam saying something about her Interact Club and all the work her members had put in at a local soup kitchen. Brian talked about "No Place Like Home" and the difference his students had made in the lives of several Louisiana families who had lost their homes to Hurricane Katrina.

I could talk about Kara's portrayal of Friar Laurence at the fall Renaissance Fair—Kara who hated to speak in front of people yet volunteered for the major part.

Paula spoke about how the city came together and worked to defeat the tax cap last fall. Next I heard Allen's voice. He was talking about Randy who took a class Allen was teaching at Strafford Learning Center, after he'd failed in the high school. "Thinking back to an English department presentation and Mr. MacKenzie talking about getting to know your students, I asked everyone to introduce themselves. When it was my turn to speak I introduced myself as Randy's uncle. It got to be a sort of joke and eventually Randy started referring to himself as my nephew. It was really kind of cool and he did great in the class."

Then it was my turn and I heard myself saying, "I had to deal with something this year I haven't had much experience with; I had a student who hated me. Bob came in every day and started out in a chair where he could lay an arm on my desk—hating me. He actually wrote on the top of a test 'I hate Mr. MacKenzie (I can say it if I want).' I tried talking to him. Nothing. He wouldn't write when we did journal writes. He wouldn't answer a question of the day, or if he did it was with 'I don't know' or a shrug of the shoulders. One day I used this writing prompt: *I hate it when . . . or I like it when . . .* I figured at the very least he could write about hating me. But when it came his time to share he said, "I got nothing." Basically whatever I was selling Bob wasn't buying. I had a meeting with his aides. No change. I had a meeting with his mom and the administration. Nothing.

I eventually found out that Bob liked to read, so I tried to see if he would like it better if I just gave him independent readings with some open ended questions. No dice. For weeks I tried and for weeks he resisted. Bob was just one of those kids who was not going to be reached—period.

Then the weirdest thing happened. The day before final exams began I went through several piles of papers on my desk, separating, tossing, filing. I finally made it to the bottom and picked up the last paper, a blank lined sheet like the kind I pass out for writing assignments. I was about to put it back in my closet for next year when I turned it over and noticed some writing. I read Bob Hanson (not his real name) in the upper corner. I glanced down and read, *I hate it when . . . people laugh at me or make fun of me, and they don't even know me.* I see quick visions of Heather and Luke and Washington and notes. "That paper, those few words, that was my greatest success of the year."

This column originally appeared in Foster's Daily Democrat, Dover, NH on June 30, 2009.

What to Teach

I'm treading again on dangerous ground here, going into situations I've never gone into before, but they're stories that I think need to be told. I won't use any real names* or dates, and I won't play the blame game, but if I am to be honest about the realities of the public school system, if I am to be the child advocate I claim to be, these are stories which need to be told.

Some of my students live in really difficult situations. Kids frequently hear adults say, "these are the best years of your lives," but for some it's just not true. For others, if it is true it's no wonder they just check out, out of school, out of family, sometimes out of life. I have students who don't get enough to eat, and are too proud to admit it or too embarrassed to apply for free or reduced meals. I have students whose parents, more likely whose *parent*, rarely if ever check to see about homework. I have had students who lived with abusive parents, alcoholic parents, and drug addicted parents.

I had a student several years ago whose best friend once told me he had listened to his buddy's mother say to all her children, "Hey, I work two jobs Monday through Friday; the weekends are *my* time, so don't bother me and don't get into any trouble." My response was, "So when is their time?"

A couple of years ago I got taken to task by a student's parents. They didn't like it that my course included literature which dealt with tough issues like rape, incest, and drug abuse. Why would I teach literature, they asked, like *The Yellow Wallpaper*, about a woman slipping through post-partum depression into insanity, or Greg Graffin's essay "Anarchy in the

Tenth Grade," that takes the reader through Graffin's adolescent world of punk, including teenage sexual activity, drug use, gothic dress, and Mohawk hairdos? They were concerned about us discussing issues of morality in association with this literature. I remember leaving the meeting and the student's dad saying to me, "Mr. MacKenzie, you should stick to reading and writing and leave teaching morality to the parents." I looked at him and said, "For your child that might be great; you probably teach and model morality as well or better than I do. But what about some of my other students for whom I might *be* the moral compass? What about my responsibility to them?"

Another time I had a conversation with a student who said to me, "My mother's a crack addict and I have no idea where my father is—I haven't seen him in years." I have a responsibility to her. Yet another student once talked about a bracelet she cherished, because it had been given to her by her father, just before he walked out of their lives—forever. And another who came in early one morning in tears needing to talk.

"My mother is threatening to throw me out of the house," she sobbed.

"But you're only seventeen," I responded. "She can't do that."

"Well, she says if I don't stop disrupting the family I'll have to move out. Mr. MacKenzie, I don't understand it; I'm a really good kid."

"I know you are, *Jane, so what do you think the problem is?" I queried.

"I don't know," she said, "I think my mother just doesn't like me."

"But Jane," I replied with a look of disbelief, "what's to not like?"

I think I do reasonably well with teaching the concepts of literary analysis, composition, and critical thinking. But it's hard to teach a kid the need to read when the more pressing need is food. It's hard to convince a kid that good writing skills are important when they graduate and get a job—if they've moved around so much and are so far behind that graduation is barely a dream. How was I supposed to get a kid to feel a part of our school, to connect with our school, when as a result of mom's addiction, DCYS, and the court system she had been in and out of three different high schools in a year-and-a-half, and when the odds were in a few weeks she'd be off to the next one? Do you think that kid really cared about the similes and metaphors in *The Odyssey*? Do you think she had any real interest in the social and cultural backdrop for Steinbeck's *Of Mice and Men*? Do you think she gave a darn about boosting her language usage skills for the upcoming Measures in Academic Progress tests, when she knew she probably wouldn't be here for them anyway?

I told you I was treading on dangerous ground, but I'm a public school teacher and *you* are the public; so are my students who worry more about getting enough to eat than getting their homework done, and those who still love their parent, even a drug addicted parent. They need a modified curriculum. I can't just teach them grammar and composition—because that's not their priority. I *may* get to some of that, but I might have to start with abandonment, neglect, abuse, or addictions first.

I once had a student who suffered from depression, and for weeks she refused to participate in almost every aspect of my class: no response to the question of the day, little if anything in her journal writes, and absolutely nothing into a class discussion. The weird thing was this kid rarely missed a word I said. When I talked she listened. We were about eight weeks into the course when we were doing a couple of character sketches on the board one day. I nearly shouted when I saw her hand go up. I nearly cried when I heard a response come out of her mouth.

This column originally appeared in Foster's Daily Democrat, Dover, NH on April 7, 2009.

Why I Write

Some people write to entertain. Others write to educate. Still others write to advise, persuade, or influence. The reason I write parallels why Tim O'Brien claims he wrote *The Things They Carried*. In one chapter O'Brien writes that "right here, now, as I invent myself, I'm thinking of all I want to tell you about why this book is written as it is. . . . I want you to feel what I felt." And when you're done reading his book—you do.

Room 217 was conceived in large part to bring you into my school, more times than not into my classroom. I want you to hear what I hear. I want you to see what I see. I want you to experience what I experience. I want you to share my happiest moments in public education and those that have become among my deepest sorrows. In short, like Tim O'Brien, I want you to feel what I feel.

I want you to feel Alyssa's pain of frustration as I asked for a fourth rewrite before I could grade a paper, so it could receive a passing grade. I want you to feel *my* pain as I watched the moisture begin to pool in her eyes.

I want you to experience my pride as Rachel told me she got accepted into her first choice college. I want you to experience Chris's pride, a recent post-grad, when he came to school to tell me he had just proposed to Athena, his high school sweetheart, and David's pride, who is working diligently to become the first in his family to go to college.

I even want you to hear the bad. I want you to hear the student call me an A-hole, or tell me point blank, "I hate you" or invite me to "Go to hell." If I'm going to be real you have to hear those things as well. But I need you to do what I do, I need you to let them go and not focus on them. You have to hear me correct all the "Me and him" statements on a daily basis. You have to see all the "their, there, and they're" problems I regularly circle in papers, and hear how many times a day I yell at some guy for his pants being belted too low or some girl for her blouse being cut too low.

The thing is if I don't tell you about the rare "Mr. MacKenzie, I hate you," the frequent "Mr. MacKenzie, I love you" has far less meaning. If I neglect to tell you I've been invited to hell, how can I explain what it meant when Luke invited me to join him at the top ten breakfast, as a favorite teacher.

I want you to know how cool it was to run into Mike the other day. I hadn't seen him in years, but I see his name every day: on the giant Scrabble board in my room, which he helped build—in 1998.

I want you beside me as I conferenced Logan's research paper with him last Friday after school for proper MLA citations, and I want you sitting with me when I was playing Cribbage with Justin and Tyler in the cafetorium this past Saturday—at 5:00 in the morning—I was chaperoning a lock-in! I want you to hear Andy tell me to go "F" myself, because I want you to hear Johnny tell me, "I'll probably graduate because of you."

All three of my classes recently finished watching Dead Poets Society as part of our poetry unit, and we were discussing the suicide of Neil Perry, one of the film's main characters. Neil had joined a theater group, against his father's wishes, and literally fell in love with acting. Following the threats and chastisement of his father when he discovered Neil's deception, Neil took his life. Our class discussions found us questioning whether or not Neil's English teacher, Mr. Keating, bore any responsibility for the death, since Mr. Keating had encouraged his students to follow their dreams and avoid conformity whenever possible. While most found no culpability on the part of Mr. Keating, some did concede that if he had not encouraged his students to follow their dreams Neil might still be alive.

After a bit we put aside the actual suicide and looked more closely at non-conformity, and choosing Frost's "less-traveled" road. I told them of a former student who was the consummate non-conformist, who liked to push the proverbial envelope and live one step closer to the edge than most. Alex believed, *if it hasn't been tried yet, someone should.* Tragically he died in a diving accident. He was not doing something stupid, just something no one else had tried. I also told them how moved I was by something his mother shared at his memorial service: "Alex, we could have clipped your wings and you would still be alive, but you would not be happy."

A few weeks ago I wrote a rather poignant column called What to Teach. In it I shared some of the difficulties with which a few of my students live. I wrote it because I wanted you to understand the challenges some of them regularly face. Shortly after it was published I ran into my friend Jim, a Somersworth School Board member. He grabbed my arm and said, "You know I wanted to punch you the other day!" Now Jim is a pretty, shall I say masculine kind of guy, but I knew there was more coming. "I was actually crying as I read your last column!" I sort of chuckled and replied, "Jim, I was crying as I wrote it."

Yup, I write because, like Tim O'Brien, I want you to feel what I feel—and at least some of you do.

This column originally appeared in Foster's Daily Democrat, Dover, NH on June 2, 2009.

What Am I Going to Do Next Year?

By the time this gets to press it will indeed be all over, including the shouting—for this year anyway. Since early June we have been busy with year-end testing, awards ceremonies, the senior class trip, the senior banquet, yearbook signings, the top ten breakfast, graduation, final exams, and probably a deal or two on the side to get that D- for a diploma. We've been through tears, cheers, silly-string, beach balls, handshakes, hugs, and photographs. Yes, the modes of congratulations were many, for both seniors and underclassmen. But those are only some of the most visible and audible parts of the end-of-the-year story.

By Thursday noontime the Student Council was hosting its annual faculty and staff barbeque (which eventually relocated and continued on into the evening at the home of one of my colleagues), and a few straggling students were taking advantage of the make-up time for finals. Teachers were beginning the "check-out" process, the tech folks were already planning their "software updates," and the custodians had started the annual cleaning out of hundreds of lockers: lecture notes, crib notes, and love notes; papers, smelly sneakers, last winter's coats, portfolios, perfume, nail polish, even deodorant; if it was still in there, it was "outa there." I'm betting we'll need an extra dumpster pick-up this week.

Clean-up continued Thursday afternoon and even into Friday. There was inventorying of books, discarding of junk, and packing up of things that went home for the summer. Some teachers were packing up permanently (like those retiring), while others were simply packing up to move (like those headed to other rooms or departments). Books and catalogs were being sorted, pictures and posters were being taken down, leftover papers, projects, and snacks—some from as far back as Christmas—were being trashed.

Then every once in a while there came through the wandering leftover student. A few *elect* to come in to check on a final exam grade or say that last good-by. Some *have* to come in, maybe to get the Transcript Request Form they either mangled or filled out wrong, or forgot to get in the first place (or maybe to grab that backpack out of a locker before the janitors toss it!). Then there are a few students, and teachers, who just come in because they find it hard to leave—I would be one of those.

Really, in a lot of ways I hate the end of the year. It's not because I'm not happy for my students, it's not because I'm jealous of those who are retiring, and it's not because I don't love having the floor of my classroom stripped and waxed. It's because I don't do change well. See, I had mostly seniors who aren't going to be here any more. Many of them I've known for their whole four years of high school. The forty-five or so I had in my class this year I got to know even better. We spent a lot of time together (ninety minutes a day, five days a week, for eighteen weeks!). We have composed together and commiserated together. We've shared letters, lectures, and literature. I've grown accustomed to their little idiosyncrasies, like who always does their homework, comes in late, or whines about being tired. I know their favorite topics for conversation and composition—and digression. I know what kind of soda they drink, who eats low-fat crackers or fruit, and who eats two bacon, egg, and cheese breakfast sandwiches, sometimes three—like it makes a lot of difference that the English muffin is *whole wheat*! I know their smiles, their grumbles, and their hugs, and who's going to share their food with me. I can tell who's prepared for the class and who's trying desperately to avoid eye contact with me without looking like they're trying to avoid eye contact with me. Do you see what I mean? I know them. I'm comfortable with them. I'm already missing them, and we haven't been out of school for twenty-four hours yet!

So I come in early and stay late a lot near the end of school. I may cover the homework lab for a friend or gather the signatures (initials actually) for our association's membership dues list, but those are just excuses, really. The truth is I don't like losing a whole set of students every year—it's hard. They have in a very real way become part of my family. I have imparted some knowledge to them (I hope) and they've imparted much to me, and many of them I'll never see again. I don't like it. But that's part of the gig. I watch other teachers deal with them for three years, then I get them, and then they're gone.

It's not *all* bad, though. I can celebrate their accomplishments with them, like Danika's record-breaking javelin throw, John's four-year, full tuition, full expenses scholarship to UNH, Derek's acceptance to Hesser College to study communication, and Caleb's most deserved "Most Improved" award for public speaking. And not only that but while I was walking around pretending to actually have a reason to be at school I found a couple of textbooks we thought were lost. I picked up an abandoned pen, a favorite kind that I'm too cheap to buy, and I was given an unopened can of Planter's honey roasted peanuts, which was very shortly no longer unopened. Still, each June I leave school on the last day wrestling with that "what am I going do next year?" feeling. But every year something happens. It's always different, it's always unexpected, and it's always good. This year it happened Thursday afternoon as I headed out the main entrance: a voice from across the front lawn hollered, "Hey Mr. Mac! You and me, block one, this September!" That's what I'm going to do next year.

This column originally appeared in Foster's Daily Democrat, Dover, NH on June 24, 2008.

PART IV

THOSE AWKWARD MOMENTS

You know the ones I'm talking about, like you're standing in front of the class—have been for quite a while—and discover your fly is down, or you're walking around the middle of the classroom, talking to your students, holding a nice juicy just pealed orange in one hand and the knife you pealed it with in the other, and as you're walking and talking you trip over the *All-Aboard* platform (2'x2'x8"), which you have failed to remember is on the floor, and down you go, with no way to brace the fall, trying to save the orange and not slice yourself, and the best you can do is end up with a scraped shin from the edge of the wood platform and a smooshed orange from the floor. Or like when you're elected to be the scribe for your group, because you are an English teacher after all, and you're writing the group's thoughts and ideas on this gigantic post-it paper, and someone in the group points out that *refering*, for example, has two "r's" in it. Or when a student who happens to know that you're an active church member, asks you, in front of the whole class, if you tithe to your church. Oh yes, I have had my share of awkward moments.

I was talking with a group of parents one night at Open House about the piece of literature we were currently reading. Trying to give it some historical context, I started talking about the social climate of the day, the fairly recently concluded Civil War . . . when all of a sudden I realized something wasn't feeling just right and it dawned on me that I was confusing, thus contextualizing, the wrong piece of literature with the wrong historical period. Can you say *awkward*?

Another time I was walking down the hall and a couple of my colleagues stopped me to chat for a minute. As we were about to part company one of them made some comment about what I was wearing. I thought it was a joke I hadn't heard correctly, so I asked what he said. He repeated, "You ought to tuck your shirt in—you're a teacher." Or how about this one? I walked into the teacher's room one day to do some early morning copying before anyone else arrived and I had to compete for the copiers. While my stuff was running I happened to notice that our local paper was open on the large center table. Then I realized what had caught my eye: it was my head shot. It was the day before's paper and it was open to my column. I then looked a little closer and realized that someone had sat there, most likely not alone, and circled every personal pronoun in the column. I mean the column is supposed to mainly focus on people, issues, and situations in *my* classroom. How would one do that without using personal pronouns? But I can tell you, it was pretty awkward.

I've had moments where students yelled at me, called me an A hole, and told me to F off. I've had moments where I embarrassed a student in class or, even worse, made them cry. Yup, I've had any number of those awkward moments. Sometimes you can ignore them or apologize. Sometimes they can help you smarten up (like switching to a plastic knife to peal oranges and putting away the All-Aboard!). Sometimes you get a chance to make them right.

The "Special" in Special Ed

Joanna was a star athlete and an excellent scholar, and was taking my Honors English III course. She was also a student who received Special Ed services. Now for those of you who don't really understand what that means, I'll tell you—briefly. Students who receive Special Ed services have been determined to have some kind of learning disability affecting how they acquire and retain information. The disability might be in hearing, sight, motor skills, attention span, or any number of other areas. It can be physical, emotional, or psychological. In short there are all kinds of learning disabilities that would qualify a student for special services, and in many cases they have nothing to do with intelligence, but only in the ability to take in and process information. The services, along with educational goals, strategies, and any necessary curriculum modifications or accommodations would then be specified in an Individual Education Plan (IEP).

As I said, along with many other special distinctions, Joanna had a learning disability, which means she had an IEP, a case manager, and a connection to the Special Ed department. I remember it was a day early in the fall semester when the Special Ed director called me and said that Joanna's mother had requested that the three of us meet. Since I love parental involvement, and because I didn't have a choice anyway, I readily agreed and we set a time. Our Special Ed director was not quite as eager for the meeting as I, and told me as much. She was concerned that "mom" was looking to push for her daughter, perhaps too hard, and most of my colleagues knew I was pretty resistant to being pushed. Convinced that there was nothing to worry about, that we all wanted what was best for Joanna, I said,

"Don't worry, everything will be fine." I know I did not allay the director's fears, but at the appointed day and time we met.

The first question from mom was, "Mr. MacKenzie, I'd like to know what accommodations you are prepared to make for my daughter?"

Okay—a bit awkward, but she gets right to the point. "I'm prepared to make the same accommodations I offer to all of my students. For example, there is no assigned seating in my class, so any student can sit where they need or want to sit. If students need to have a drink or something to eat, that is not a problem— ninety minutes is a long class. Homework assignments are given orally and in writing. Major assignments include an assignment sheet, a rubric, and I typically share the work of former students or my own work as examples. And for identified students, if their IEP provides for it, any tests or quizzes may be taken in the study center." I took a breath and awaited a response.

"What about modifications on the length of major papers?"

Now I know where at least part of her concerns are. "Well, remember that this is an honors class, so I don't think I can reasonably modify the length. I assign 5-7 page papers because that's what they're going to have to write in college. But she can always rewrite a paper if she is not happy with the grade."

"What do you mean?"

"I mean that when the paper comes back if she is not happy with the grade, she should read my comments carefully, ask about anything she doesn't understand, and then rewrite the paper. Assuming the grade goes up, and it almost always does, I simply erase the old grade and write in the new one."

"Really?"

"Absolutely. She can do that as many times as she likes until she achieves the grade she is looking for. And that is not just for her—I do that for all of my students. As long as they are willing to keep writing I'm willing to keep reading. If learning is the ultimate objective, they're learning almost by default."

"Well that's very interesting, and I like that concept—a lot. But what you may not know is that my daughter may have rewritten that paper three or four times before you got it the first time—and then received a 'C.'"

"I see—and was she unhappy with the 'C'?" I queried.

"Devastated," came the reply. "I mean she absolutely loves your class—she talks about it all the time, but she is putting in an incredible amount of work on your papers."

"Then maybe we need to be convincing your daughter that if a 'C' is the very best she can do, then a 'C' is good enough."

Was mom a tad pushy? Maybe. Was I a bit rigid? It's possible. And I know my poor Special Ed director was on edge during the entire exchange. Yes, there were a few moments that got a little awkward, but for the most part it was a good, rewarding exchange. We both recognized that we wanted the same thing— the absolute best for a very special young lady. And we ended up pretty good friends to boot. She never missed parent conferences and she was always at Joanna's sporting events. We never bumped into each other at school without a warm greeting. She wrote supportive notes and never missed an opportunity to thank me for all I did for Joanna, and I have always respected her unyielding advocacy for her child. I wish more parents actively advocated for their children's education—regular and special ed.

And how did Joanna react to all this pushing, prodding, and advocating? I worried a little bit—I paid closer attention to how hard she was working and how many rewrites she was doing— until I read what she wrote in my yearbook: *I can't believe how much you have taught me in just one year . . . I'm really looking forward to your Honors English IV class.*

This column originally appeared in Foster's Daily Democrat, Dover, NH on April 26, 2007.

Dealing with "Tone"

I hesitate to admit this, being an English teacher, but we are currently in my least favorite unit of my freshmen English class. See English I is basically a survey course in that it covers small parts of a number of different areas in the academic discipline of English: short story, nonfiction, poetry, drama, the epic, and the novel. My least favorite is poetry. I don't know exactly why except that it's probably because I feel least comfortable with it. No, I think I actually feel inept with poetry. Take my piano playing, for instance. I am pretty comfortable with sitting down and playing most any song as long as I have the music. But I'm not going to sit down and whip off a Beethoven sonata. For me, poetry is sort of piano's Beethoven; you know what I mean?

Anyway, the other day, while in our poetry unit we were talking about the rhetorical device of "tone," or the author's *attitude* toward his or her subject. For example, if I were writing a poem, highly unlikely but one never knows, about winter or snow you can be pretty sure the tone would be negative—I HATE being cold. However, if I were writing about the Red Sox the tone would likely be one of awe, or wonder, or respect, or just plain envy!

For more concrete examples we could argue that Poe displayed an attitude of deep worry or concern for the soul of his lost Lenore in "The Raven." Robert Frost, on the other hand, certainly conveyed optimism in "The Road Not Taken," while Robert Graves in "The Face in the Mirror" reveals a certain self-respect or dignity, even as the mirror reveals the "crookedly broken nose," the "coarse grey hair," and the "forehead, wrinkled and high" of old age.

After working with several pieces of poetry and examining them through the lens of "tone" I asked each of my students to write their own poem (if you just heard a groan it was not imagined) paying special attention to tone, to be sure the piece allowed their attitude toward the subject to come through. Samantha wrote about caring for her "Kitty," from the meow and scratch at the door, to toweling it off, to feeding it, petting it, and then repeating it. Lizzie chose to write about love, beginning "Love is an emotion that has no season / It is seldom even based on reason." She talked about the unconditional and unpredictable aspects of love, and the necessity to share love. She concluded with "So if you possess this gift from above / Look up to the heavens and thank God for love." And Andrew looked to the seasons of nature speaking of the hot days of summer, the return to school in the fall, the long cold and short holiday decorations of winter. He went on to write: "Spring is here / People are happy / Flowers peaking out of the Earth / Trees refilling with leaves / The world just brightened up." I'm guessing he liked spring best.

One of the funniest and perhaps the most revealing came from Kyle.

Kyle's an interesting guy. He has long, bushy black hair, a fairly stocky build, and just a touch of wise-guy behind a typically smiling and affable face. Now it so happened that on this particular day Kyle was late to class.

"I was in the caf," came the response to my query about his tardiness.

"Excuse me?" I replied, thinking my look sufficiently conveyed my annoyance.

"I was in the caf," he responded again, with an I-just-told-you-that attitude.

"And you were in the caf because . . .?" I pushed.

"I was thirsty," he returned, with a sly smile.

"Were you really? Well you can be thirsty with me for an hour after school tomorrow!"

He gave me another look and then sat down. A couple of minutes later I noticed him open his backpack and I saw the oversized can of Iced Tea come out. Now the sly smile was mine— "Don't even think about opening that" I blurted, as I hopped out of my chair, grabbed the can, and set it down out of his reach. "Now get started on your poem."

The next day, having finished them for homework, I asked who would be willing to share their poem with the class. I was pleasantly surprised to see Kyle's hand go up and acknowledged him. This is his work:

Drink of the Heavens

Taken away at beginning of day
Oh I long for my Iced Tea
Although it is here yet not so near
That drink has captured me!

Late for third block then door was locked
Oh I long for my Iced Tea
Mr. Mac is there but he doesn't care
Oh how he glares at me!

I sit in my seat as he begins to repeat
How I shouldn't be late for class.
When he starts shaking the Earth begins quaking
If only I'd brought a pass!

Who would have known it'd sit on a throne
That Arizona Iced Tea
I still can't believe the gods could conceive
Something so blessed be!

It was good. It was funny. It conveyed his frustration. It not only revealed tone but also had a consistent rhyme scheme and meter. And it more than met the length requirement! Good grief, if I had known that from my throne I could conjure such work out of him I'd have been more aggravating sooner.

Come to think of it, Kyle plays the guitar. Maybe he could aggravate me into learning a Beethoven sonata . . . or not. No, much as I liked it Kyle's poem didn't make me feel any more comfortable writing poetry, but it sure did make me wonder what he might have done if he'd been hungry too, and bought say a sausage, egg, and cheese croissant!

This column originally appeared in Foster's Daily Democrat, Dover, NH on November 15, 2007.

A Vocabulary Lesson

I really hope that the primary job of a teacher, at least in secondary education and beyond, is to recognize talent within our students and then do everything possible to help them develop that talent. For example, I love it when I say to a student who is a bit too abstract in his writing, "Okay, take this line right here; take a picture of it and then give me as many details as you can. Tell me exactly what the picture looks like." And then with a blink their 15 watt eyes power up to 60 as they reply, "I think I can do that." *I'm sure you can.* I love it even more when I am reading a student's paper and find myself thinking *Wow, that's really good; I wish I'd written that.* I've long said I sometimes wonder who is teaching whom, for I learn at least as much from my students as they do from me. Maybe I should be paying them.

Now I acknowledge there are those who think we teachers are little more than social engineers, that we spend too much time espousing our political ideologies, that our classes focus too heavily on trying to advance our leftist social agenda with little if any time spent on academics. Let me assure you, such is not the case in my classroom. First of all I don't espouse my political views any more than my students espouse theirs—at my urging. I don't care what their views are so much as I care that they know why they have them. Secondly, I am a right-of-center Republican, so if I have a social agenda it's a conservative one. In my English classes we spend a lot of time on academics. In fact, I drive my students crazy with proper formatting and documentation, with sentence construction and ordering of paragraphs, with peer conferencing, the writing process, thesis statements, even good old-fashioned grammar.

One day a few years ago, in Honors English IV, we were doing an in-class reading assignment. As usual we were going over the vocabulary words in context as we got to them, and I noticed that one of the underlined words was "tithe." I was a bit surprised that it would be considered a new word for seniors but I threw it out to the class anyway. Not one hand went up when I queried for its definition, not even a hand I had expected. See I knew that one of my students, Josh, was an active member of his church and their youth group, for we had had many discussions about his goal to be a full-time youth pastor after he graduated college. But not even Josh's hand went up to define "tithe."

"Nobody knows what the word 'tithe' means? Josh, no idea?"

"Well, I know I've heard it before at church, but I can't give you a definition."

So I began to explain. "I don't know exactly what Miriam Webster has to say but according to the Bible a tithe is the ten percent of your income that you are expected to give back to God. The idea is that all things you receive you receive from God and the tithe is the portion you must give back in some form. Most major religions suggest that members tithe through their local church and its related charities." "And," I went on, "biblically speaking, the tithe is the *first* ten percent of that with which you have been blessed, not whatever is left over. It is the minimum expectation. If you want to make an offering, the offering is what you give above and beyond the tithe." I sort of enjoyed seeing lips drawn slightly apart and quizzical expressions as I looked around the room.

"Any questions before we move on?" I asked. "Yes, Josh," I said as I saw his hand go up.

"Mr. MacKenzie, do you tithe?"

Now my students all know, from any number of discussions on various pieces of religious literature, that I am an active member of my church, so I immediately realize, as my face begins to get warm, that I have about two seconds to make a decision. I can embarrass myself greatly. Or I can lie. I decide to tell the truth.

"No, Josh, I don't," I say, just a bit more quietly.

Now any decent person can usually tell, by both sight and sound, when they have put someone in an uncomfortable position, and leave "bad enough" alone.

"Why not?"

Thank you so much Josh, my mind whispers as it tries to buy some thinking time, my face going from Rosé to Merlot.

"I can't really give you an answer you'll like, Josh."

"What do you mean"

God, Joshua, cut me some slack will ya?

"I don't know, I guess I just never thought I could afford to tithe." *Now please, get off this!*

"How do you figure that?"

Jeezum, Josh, give me a break!

"You know, every time I've looked at our income I've thought, gosh that would be a lot of money—I can't give ten percent!"

Of course I realized as soon as the words were out of my mouth just how stupid they sounded. By that rationale, what the heck was I saying about the ninety percent!

"You know what, Josh, I don't have a good reason to give you."

That afternoon when I got home I called the church office and doubled our pledge.

Hey, folks. I can't tell you how many of those students remember the proper format for MLA pagination, or what constitutes a good thesis statement, or how to *show* instead of *tell* a main point. I don't know how many remember correct pronoun usage, or how to properly cite a source, or when to use "whom" instead of "who." But I'll just bet you that most of them remember the definition of "tithe;" I know I sure do.

This column originally appeared in Foster's Daily Democrat, Dover, NH on October 26, 2006.

Eye Contact

I hurt a student's feelings the other day. I didn't do it on purpose or anything, it just sort of happened. Like when you're checking out at Walmart or someplace and your credit card fouls up—you tick off everyone behind you while you turn red, exclaiming tersely how there must be some mistake and frantically search for another card, all the while wondering if you have enough cash should all else fail. You don't mean for it to happen—it just does. Well, that's how I hurt Jared's feelings—we had a kind of glitch with the Honors English IV credit card.

We were doing our usual round-the-room this Monday morning and when I got to Jared he said whatever he said about the weekend and then remarked, "Hey, by the way, why did you call me Saturday?" We stared at each other benignly for a few seconds while I went rewinding through my weekend. "You know," I finally replied, "I don't remember—why did I call you Saturday?" Our eyes remained locked for several more seconds and then it came to me. "Oh yeah, I remember now. Hang on a second." With just a glint of playful sarcasm I reached for my rank book and started turning pages to the right block.

"Ah, yes. Jared, can you explain to me how you have managed to get a zero on three out of the four *Tuesdays with Morrie* quizzes and a check minus on the fourth?" I poked.

"I . . . don't know," he responded slightly flushed.

"What do you mean you don't know?" I pushed, "you're a senior honors student. How can you not know?"

"Well, I guess I obviously didn't do the reading," he pushed back, a bit of a quiver in his syllables and embarrassment in his cheeks.

Now I should have stopped there, but I didn't. See I have this problem, and I confess it in advance to every class I teach. I put so much of myself into each course I develop, the papers I assign and the literature I include in the syllabus, that I take my classes personally—maybe to a fault. I tell them, "When you blow off the readings or other homework assignments, I don't feel like you're blowing work off I feel like you're blowing *me* off." I know I shouldn't feel that way but I do. So I kept up the pressure.

"I see. And can you make me understand why a very capable senior honors student near the top of his class chose *not* to do some simple readings in a book that is a major component of this unit?" I jabbed, my own color rising by this time.

"Ah, I probably can't in a way that would satisfy you," the bit of a quiver now a pronounced tremolo (though I must say, he never broke eye contact with me during the entire exchange), "but you could have talked to me about this in private instead of making me feel worthless in front of the whole class . . ."

I *hate* it when that happens—when I behave more like a student than the students do. So after a really loud, awkward silence I got up from my seat, walked to my computer and continued conversing while I popped in a disk, brought up a file, and clicked *print.* "Worthless—you think I was suggesting you're worthless?"

"Well, that's sure what it felt like," he claimed.

"Let me ask you something," I said as I picked up the Word document from the printer tray and walked back towards my seat. "You remember the Teacher Reference you asked me to write for you last fall? Well, normally I bring them right to Guidance and students don't see them, but if you'll give me permission I'd like to read yours now—in front of the whole class, where I've obviously managed to embarrass the both of us—just so there will be no question as to what I really think of you. May I?"

"Sure, what the heck," he replied, only a trace of skepticism still lingering in his stare.

I began reading:

While I have had opportunities to see Jared on the basketball court and the baseball field, this semester's Honors English IV course is the first time I have been privileged to have him in class. My limited experience with him thus far shows him to be both an athlete and a scholar: unpretentious but highly skilled, quiet but usually prepared to participate, respectful and greatly respected.

Academically, Jared has quickly made his presence known in my classroom. He is not the top achiever in his class but he is a top student. He is typically conscientious about his academic responsibilities. He is willing to work with and share with the people around him. Because of his eye contact I know that whenever I am talking Jared is not missing a word. His grades so far have been very good but his presence has been even better.

Perhaps the most important thing I can offer about Jared is the impression he has made on me as a person. In discussing "first encounters" one day Jared told of his first encounter with me—a compliment I gave him following last year's semi-final baseball game. I then told of my first memory of him—his talking about the great relationship he has with his older brothers. Jared's personal narrative was about one of those brothers and his children, one of whom is two-year-old Olivia, who tries so hard to say Uncle Jared but can only get out Kull Jaaaweeed! I have no doubt Jared will be a great scholar and very successful in his secondary and post-secondary pursuits. I have even less doubt Jared will be a great human being.

When I finished reading I looked up at Jared and said, "You . . . ? Worthless?" And we both had to break eye contact.

This column originally appeared in Foster's Daily Democrat, Dover, NH on October 12, 2006.

Captains

I have to confess—I like having fun in my classes. Not only do I think learning can be fun, I think it should be fun. No, I don't mean we should spend our entire class time cracking jokes or partying. Neither do I want to dread coming to class, and I'm pretty sure my students don't want to either. So while we're learning about Shakespeare, and gerunds, and *The Things They Carried*, and "then" and "than," I think we should have some fun, and we should definitely avoid ruts. I don't like driving in them, I don't like slipping into them, and I certainly don't like teaching in them. So just in case I'm not "fun" enough or "original" enough all by myself, or in case I slip into a routine, every once in a while I toss in a game. There is a game of Balderdash that lives in the bottom drawer of my filing cabinet. I also made up this game we play on the whiteboard that's kind of a cross between Wheel of Fortune and Hangman, only there is no wheel, or fortune, or buying of vowels, and there are no stick bodies getting hung from a gallows one stick-limb at a time. And then on the back wall of my classroom there is a giant Scrabble board—that tends to be the favorite.

Now since I am a fun loving kind of guy, and since most of my students are relatively mature seniors, there aren't too many things that I have to prohibit in my classes. In fact I list the few basic things in my syllabus: No making fun of or laughing at other students; no plagiarism; no foul language. Oh there are a few others that I talk about as things come up, like don't write about things that are so personal you can't stand for anybody else to read them, because somebody else will, whoever you're peer conferencing with for one. Also, don't write about illegal activities, since, frankly, I don't want to know about them. And don't write about your sex life, because in my opinion you shouldn't have one. Beyond that, I don't say "no" a lot—most anything else is at least open to negotiation.

So it's an early release day, November's I think, and the kids have been bugging me for over a week about playing a game of Scrabble. So after we get done with the question of the day I say, "Okay, get out the Scrabble stuff and count off by fours."

"Hey, Mr. MacKenzie! Can we pick captains and choose teams this time?" somebody asked.

I thought about it for a second, about what good kids they were, about how little they asked for and how rarely they whined. I thought about how much they liked me and I them. I thought about another time I had been asked this question . . .

I was teaching a fourth grade music class at St. Mary Academy. We had about twenty minutes left and I agreed to let them play a game we called Encore. It's a game where I put a word on the board and each group has to sing a line or two from as many songs as they can think of that contain my word. The group that sings the most songs per word gets a point and the group with the most points at the end of the class wins.

"Count off by fours," I say.

"Mr. MacKenzie, can we pick captains and choose our own teams this time?"

"Oh, all right," I respond, "but we have to go quickly."

I chose the captains and watched them go through the process of picking teams. They were pretty efficient and when they got down to just Melissa and Joey I got my first word up on the board, and as soon as they were done we began.

At the end of class, on her way out of the room, Melissa came up to me and said, rather softly, "Mr. MacKenzie, I don't really like it when we have captains pick the teams because nobody ever wants to pick me." I looked at her for a moment, the body of innocence—a young girl, intelligent, eager to learn and offer herself to the world—but the face of experience. I saw eyes resigned to the back row at contests, the front row on school busses, the chairs at dances; eyes which told more than the mouth ever would. I looked into those eyes, eyes almost but not quite void of emotion, and in their resignation saw another child, an adolescent little boy looking back at me through a 1960s mirror. Gym class with teachers who loved to have the best athletes be captains and pick the teams for basketball, or softball, or kickball or whatever ball season it was. I was almost always picked last, unless Kenneth happened to be in my gym class that year, and then I was picked next to last.

I refocused back to Melissa's eyes and said, "You know what, Melissa, I don't like it either, and we'll never do it again."

"Ahh, hello! Mr. Mac"

". . . Huh? I mean what?"

"How about it, can we pick captains and choose our own teams?"

". . . Nope. Count off by fours."

This column originally appeared in Foster's Daily Democrat, Dover, NH on September 26, 2006.

Mercy According
to Crutcher

Yesterday was one of those days. You know, when things seem to start off just fine and then turn to . . . you get the picture.

Well, things did start off great. My block two class had planned an early breakfast and I remembered my griddle and microwave. The kids also remembered their stuff (most of them anyway) and we feasted on my famous French toast and bacon. I also remembered to bring my Secret Santa gifts for some of our students down to Pam's room for wrapping. That was it for "great."

Shortly after block two began I got the "weather" notice that we would be dismissing early, never a good thing for somebody as anal as I am about plans and schedules and such. See I teach two sections of the same course during blocks one and two. Now block two would be messed up. By the time block three, my freshmen, came in . . . forget it.

During the last two-and-a-half hours I was in the building I managed to tick off one of my favorite students, barked at one of my favorite colleagues, snipped at another, lost only my second game of Cribbage ever to a student, and had to give Sharon Lampros, my principal, 25¢ for using the word "freaking," when I was cutting it up with a friend in the guidance office.

I laughed and said, "Sharon, *I* allow substitutes!"

She laughed and said, "Stephen, *I* don't. Now, hand it over!"

If you're not quite seeing what I mean yet, let me give you a few more details. I didn't just "tick off" that student, I yelled at her, and even that may be slightly downplaying what I actually did. Then when I was done yelling at her in class, I held her after class and yelled some more. Now, I wasn't yelling for no reason but that's not the point. Yelling is not a very effective tool for motivating, not for me and probably not for other teachers either. Besides, it puts me in a mood I don't want to be in, and then carries over to other situations that have absolutely nothing to do with it, like later when I barked at the one colleague and snipped at the other—about Sunday night volleyball of all things.

Well, fortunately the day finally ended. I collected up the armloads of schoolwork, briefcase, small appliances, and lunch pail (most of it untouched from the screwed up schedule), made my way out to my truck, dumped all the stuff, started it up, and froze my way home.

Finally, though I was still stewing about my lousy day, I collapsed into my recliner and picked up my latest Chris Crutcher book. I've been on a Crutcher jag for a while now. I first met him, literarily speaking, in the summer of 1998 when I taught summer school at Exeter High. I had a student there who asked me if I'd ever read *Staying Fat for Sarah Byrnes*, as he had just finished it and really liked it. Since I'd found him to be a less-than-enthusiastic student, I immediately wanted to know what kind of *book* could turn this kid on. I found out in a hurry and promptly introduced it to English II at Somersworth High, where it became an instant hit. Of course since I haven't taught English II for years, I now wish it was on the English I list. Oh well.

Anyway, last summer I read Crutcher's *Whale Talk*. This fall I read his most recent book, *Deadline*, and subsequently bought almost everything the guy's written over the last twenty-plus years. I was in the final pages of *Ironman* when I crashed into my chair and began to read. The words were the final thoughts of the facilitator of an anger management group to his member students:

"This group has taught me more about the nature of mercy than I've

learned since the night I sat in a dark room upstairs in my house and decided not to end my own life . . . I think not many people understand the nature of mercy, because it gets misnamed a lot . . . but I see it as the only medicine available for what ails us, so I need to prescribe it. It is the only medicine for our anger, it is the only medicine for our hurt, it is the only medicine for our desperation . . . . The nature of mercy allows for all things. It excuses nothing, but it allows for all things. It allows for a young man full of drink to push his luck and explode his universe, it allows for a son to stand in disobedience before his father, an' it allows for a man's meanness in trying to break that son's spirit in the name of fatherhood . . . . It allows for all things [it] don't excuse any of 'em."

--Crutcher

It wasn't exactly appropriate to my situation, but it wasn't inappropriate either, and it sure got me to thinking—and to applying. If mercy allows all things then it allows some kids to have less than others at Christmas. It also allows Secret Santas. It allows a favorite student to be annoying, and it allows the teacher to respond poorly. It allows that same teacher to nip and bite at colleagues he loves, and it allows them to be busy during the Christmas season. It allows a student to be lazy and not make use of his abilities. It also allows an author to reach out from a book and motivate that student through his fiction, and it allows a teacher to be inspired by it all. Yup, mercy allows OCD and students to beat teachers at card games and substitute words for swears (or not!). I trust it also allows redemption.

This column originally appeared in Foster's Daily Democrat, Dover, NH on January 6, 2009.

PART V

FEEDBACK . . .

There is little that helps a student improve his or her work more than good, solid feedback. Giving a paper back with an A and no meaningful feedback is about as useless to a student as giving back a paper with an F and no feedback. Feedback is what lets the student know what is strong as well as what's weaker or needs improvement for subsequent assignments. My wife often speaks of a college professor she had who graded on a scale— literally a set of scales. Yup, you read right, he weighed the papers. So what did students do? They found the heaviest paper they could. They added all kinds of fluff. They inflated bibliographies. They inserted blank pages between chapters or sections. They got nothing back! No feedback at all.

One of the most useful and memorable pieces of feedback I got during my undergrad at UNH came from Bob Connors in an advanced essay course. I can't tell you how many times I have used his advice when conferencing a paper with a student and we come to an abstract phrase. We were conferencing one of my papers and Bob said, "Okay, Steve, look at this phrase you wrote about *my cluttered room*. I want you to take a picture of that phrase and then describe everything you see in the photo." That is now one of the tools I use with my students, and the rewrites are almost always significantly better.

I wrote a column once which featured one of my AP students, one with whom I had been particularly close. I wrote about all the ways in which he personified the student most of us would kill to have in our classrooms. He was highly motivated. He was so *not* ruled by what others—any others—thought about him: his personality, his wardrobe, or his social skills (especially his lack thereof!). This kid defined "take me as I am or don't take me at all—your choice." This was a student I loved—and who without question loved me, and the column made that infinitely clear. Yet, one of the email responses I got to the column said something like this: "Dear Mr. MacKenzie, I read your column English and Alex with interest. I, too, taught high school English for many years and I would never dream of eating in class. Have things changed that much?" Yup, from all the fun, emotion, laughter, and admiration I packed into that column, the thing this reader provided me feedback on was the fact that I was eating apples in class. Interesting, don't ya think?

I had a sophomore once who wrote in his personal narrative that while on the way to his grandmother's house for Thanksgiving he "sat in the back seat staring out the window, just taking in the scenery." I gave him the "take a picture of this phrase," feedback. This is what I got the second time around: "I sat in the back seat staring out the window for most of the trip, taking in the snow covered trees, the water rushing around icy boulders in a stream that ran beside the road for several miles. I could almost feel the cold of it all, even inside the warm car." Not too bad for a sophomore, huh?

Early in my career I had a junior honors student who wasn't too wild about feedback. I gave him back his first paper and he took a few minutes to read through my comments. Shortly thereafter he approached my table, slapped the paper down in front of me, and said, "First of all MacKenzie, my writing is my writing. And second of all, you have no right to tell me how to say things." Burning though I was, I looked at him square in the eye and calmly replied, "First of all it's *Mr.* MacKenzie, and second of all, what then, in your opinion, would be my role as teacher?" I could have justifiably written up the young man—and made an enemy. Instead, I made a friend, because he immediate responded, "You know what, you're right Mr. MacKenzie, and I don't know why I spoke to you that way—my parents raised me better than that and I'm sorry."

So how did I respond when I got the feedback about eating in class? I did not fire back an immediate response in anger or dismay. I slept on it, and the next morning I sent the following: "Dear reader, I munch on something throughout most of the morning, virtually every day, and many of my students do the same. I guess things have changed that much."

In Gratitude

Every weekday morning when I awake I start thinking, almost immediately, about my kids and what we'll be doing that day. I wonder what Cooch will have to say during our regular 7:00 AM chat, and if Christopher will walk in with his typical smile and Waist Watchers grapefruit soda. I think about Leslie packing her pomegranate and Heather breaking apart her banana into chunks. I worry about telling Joe I didn't get to the CD he burned for me—again. I think about working out a pizza lunch with my freshmen and cooking breakfast for my seniors before the semester ends, and how it's ending fast!

I get particularly reflective during the Thanksgiving/Christmas/New Year's period (the *holiday* season for you politically correct types!). I don't think so much about what I do for my kids as what they do for me: Bobby, whose *mother* wanted me to have a Christmas gift; Tyler, who waited until the room emptied before giving me his container of homemade fudge. I also think about my colleagues and how much they add to my life: Paula, who asked me early in the fall if I'd proof-read her Master's papers; Sharon, who for ten years was right across the hall from me and who stopped in almost every morning with a greeting and a hug; Sheila's annual Christmas card; Joanne, whose gift of scented oil was unlike any other; Jimmy, whose support of me as department head has meant so much; Anita, who dropped off her leftover "haystacks" candy on her way home the Friday before Christmas because she knows I love them.

Yes, I think about my colleagues a lot, past and present, because I have had and do have some great ones! I called Pam, Tammy, *and*

146

Wendy one Saturday morning because I had a nagging computer question. I'll never forget Jenn, who once had the room right next to mine. She'd come swishing into school every morning, often with a peasant print skirt hanging below a long winter coat, arms laden with "stuff," looking like a cross between an aristocrat and a baglady. I remember some of our political "discussions," and giving our student Iris a single-stem iris for her birthday. I have missed her since her death, and yet, as I mentioned at her memorial gathering several years ago, we really never should have been friends at all: I am a Republican, she was a Democrat; I'm a United Methodist, she was a Quaker; I'm a low heat conservative, she was a searing liberal; I would never put a bumper sticker on my car, hers was held together with them. And yet we shared this love of literature and writing and kids and education and each other.

I was thinking about these things and more as I went to school two days after Christmas to water my plants. Along with my wilting Spath lilies I found a card from Nick, an English colleague, saying he'd miss me in the coming months when I'm away. I recalled the "Holiday" party at Dana and Sean's new house. I thought about Brian frequently calling my room at about 6:30 AM inviting me down for coffee and "dog-nuts," about Joe, Dana, and me debating mandatory seatbelt and parental notification laws for our debating classes, and Jimmy and me debating the Iraq war. I chuckled remembering Donna, Paula, Sharon, Anita, and me lip-syncing Diana Ross and the Supremes one year for a pep rally—in full costume! I thought about a counselor, Kathy, who when it comes to kids has the patience of Saint Augustine, the wisdom of Martin Luther King, and the heart of Mother Theresa; about our librarian, Cynthia, who amazes me with what sources she can dig up for my students and their research papers, or the Special Ed department and their fierce advocacy for students with learning disabilities. I have colleagues who give dozens of hours annually to PBIS teams, math teams, student leadership and peer mediation groups, and many others. Selfishly, I miss my neighbor across the hall, but she's making great strides as our new Assistant Principal.

Yes, I have some great students, but some incredible colleagues as well. When my mother died almost ten years ago, Gail suggested the student council might want to send flowers—theirs was the first arrangement I saw at the funeral home. When my wife retired both my principal and superintendent supported my request for a half-time contract.

The fact is I don't know where I could have worked for the last eleven years and felt more valued, more cared for, more supported, more loved than I have at Somersworth High School. I was in emotional agony when my student Adam died a few years ago. Following his memorial service and my eulogy, Terry, one of the patriarchs at Somersworth High, sought me out to say, "Steve, I don't know how you could have done that any better. Your words were perfect—exactly what we all needed to hear." I doubt he will ever know how much *I* needed *his* words.

A couple of days ago I went skiing with Travis, a 2005 graduate. When we hit the lodge for a last cup of cocoa I opened my lunch bag to see what I could find—I found Anita's haystacks! In a little while when I go downstairs to warm up my coffee I'll smell Joanne's soft-scented oil floating through my kitchen. Someday soon I'm going to enjoy a pork pie Paula made for me. This coming Wednesday we'll all head back to school. Pomegranates are out of season but bananas aren't, and I'll have an earful for and from Cooch. I'll have even fewer days to get in a pizza luncheon and French toast breakfast, but I made it through Joe's "Mother 1 & 2 (Earthbound)" CD! You know, life just doesn't get any better than this!

This column originally appeared in Foster's Daily Democrat, Dover, NH on January 3, 2008.

Count Your Blessings

Now and again a student, or a former student, will bless my life with something totally unexpected. My first year in Somersworth the senior class officers asked me to be guest speaker at their graduation. Some years later Pete stood at my door crying over a note of congratulations I had written him. Steve stopped me one day while walking to my truck and said, "Hey, Mr. MacKenzie, I listed you as my favorite teacher—even though I've never had you. A while ago Heather brought me a chocolate orange. You actually peal off the foil "skin" and break apart the chocolate sections!

One of those "totally unexpected" blessings was a letter from Kyle, a graduate who had not gotten into UNH and had that *what do I do now?* feeling, like Al Gore must have had after all the votes, legal opinions, and hanging chads had been counted. So Kyle came in to school and we talked. I eventually offered, "if you want UNH and you can't get in the traditional way, try a non-traditional way. Show them you're capable of more than your transcripts suggest, that you're now a different person and a different student. Register for some courses through the Division of Continuing Education, any high school graduate can do that, and get good grades. A's would be nice; B's are essential." A few months later I received this letter:

Dear Mr. MacKenzie

I am in a classroom I have never been in before surrounded by people I have never met before. Admittedly I am quite terrified. It is my first day of college life, one which I will certainly never forget. Maybe it is because I was five minutes late for my first day of Intro to Psychology because I could not find a parking spot. Or maybe it is because I left Hetzel Hall after visiting Chris to discover my car had been towed, and that I needed to pay $75.00 to have it returned. Maybe it is because I will never forget the shouting match that followed with the parking monitor. Surely these things would qualify as "unforgettable." Yet when I am asked later on that night by my parents and girlfriend "how was your first day at UNH?" these are not the first things I mention. Instead, I tell them about Pat Smith, my new English 401 teacher. Arguably my favorite and strongest subject in high school, English was the one class in college I was sure to succeed in (I do feel, however, that psychology is right up my alley). What could stand in my way? That is why I mention Pat Smith, who is just under seven feet tall, who sticks out vividly even midst the variety of people I saw throughout the day, whose cat eye glasses and purple hair immediately separate her from any other teacher I have ever seen. But what truly makes Pat Smith different is that *she* is a *he*.

When this was first announced to my class I expected to scan the room and see shocked faces. Certainly laughter would follow. Yet I saw nothing, no changes in anyone's expressions. No one cared at all. At that moment I realized, despite being ten or fifteen minutes from home, I was a *long* way from Somersworth. Now I am not prejudice, at least I try not to be, but this was a bit too much. I feared the worst. How could I overlook this and not let it interfere with how I judged the teacher, judged the class, judged the material. After all, this is my new teacher and I will therefore be subject to her/his grading. This new challenge to be open-minded was all that occupied my thoughts throughout the day and the following weekend, until I purchased the books for class.

Our first assignment was to read pages 3-43 in Anne Lamott's book *Bird by Bird*. "Great," I thought, "A book about writing, this should be exciting." But as I began reading I became pleasantly surprised. This book wasn't the dull read I thought it would be, and it was also helpful. Then I saw it—the chapter title—words that made me feel at home, that let me know everything would be okay: "Shitty First Drafts."

In a second my fears for the term turned to enthusiasm. This was material I knew. This was material I was familiar with. This was material given to me by Mr. MacKenzie. And suddenly it occurred to me that I had not thanked you. I had not thanked you for being a great teacher who I can safely say has helped me be a better writer and overall student. I had not thanked you for your motivation that helped me get back to school. I had not thanked you for giving my mom an extreme sense of pride in her son at graduation for your mere mentioning of my name in your speech. And I have not thanked you for just being you.

That is why I am writing—to show you how much I appreciate all you have done for me. Thank you for helping me get my college career started in the right direction, for without you I would not be attending school at all. Thank you for helping me not be so closed minded about life in general. This letter is a small token to show you what you are doing is worth while, and let you know you have had a positive impact on my life.

Best of luck,
Kyle

Like Pete, I cried as I reread this. What do *I* do now? Well, fortunately I don't have to leave town and start a new career as a global warming activist. I think I'll just grab a Kleenex, count my blessings, and go find that chocolate orange I've been saving.

This column originally appeared in Foster's Daily Democrat, Dover, NH on December 20, 2007.

Will You Write Me a Letter of Reference?

Sounds like a reasonable enough request, doesn't it—*will you write me a letter of reference?* And it is a reasonable request. Most years it is reasonable to some two dozen students—many years even more!

Seniors pursuing college typically ask some of their teachers to write a "teacher reference," which goes to guidance. Less frequently a student will ask a teacher to write a full letter of recommendation which goes directly into their application packet. The former is a brief sketch of a given student, usually solicited from the three staff members who best know him or her. The latter is just what it indicates, a formal letter on behalf of the student printed on school letterhead.

This year I've done about twelve teacher references and five formal letters, and the season is not nearly over. I'm probably good for at least that many again. By the time I'm done I'll have around fifteen hours of work into them. I'm not complaining, though, because I kind of enjoy doing it—even when I don't have time, which is pretty much always. The best part is it forces me to think hard about the person for whom I am writing. I search through my memory, their student work folders, and any pictures I may have. I think, I type, I smile, recalling the very best of my relationship with that student. For maybe a half-hour I am in deep, concentrated mental companionship with that someone—he or she has my undivided attention as I put into words all the things that make him or her special to me. Best of all I get to think about only their positives, never the flaws. It really is quite cool!

The time is especially intense for the formal letters, because with them there's no sharing of risk; it's all me. I'm the only one on that page who is helping or hurting the student's chances of acceptance. I tell them when they ask for the letter that I want to be an asset not a liability. I tell them that my letters tend to be rather unconventional and if, when I'm done, they're not happy with it I'll revise it, or they can just chuck it altogether. I also say, "Realize that my guiding principle in letters of recommendation is to write what I believe shows the very best of you and your experiences here at Somersworth High." Sometimes the "best" I write about includes evidence of learning from struggles, like when I wrote about a student losing an election, or the one who got caught cheating, or the student who failed a course. I haven't had one trashed yet.

This year I was asked for a letter by a former student. She had graduated from an associate's program—with honors by the way—and was ready to head toward a bachelor's degree. Having remained close friends since her graduation I immediately knew some of what I would write. When I asked she said she trusted me. I guess she did because this is what ultimately went into her UNH application packet:

Ladies and gentlemen,

I have been asked to write any number of letters of reference and recommendation over the years, but never have I been more pleased or proud to comply than I am now. Grace Johnson (not her real name) was a student at Somersworth High several years ago where I was fortunate enough to meet her, and we became friends. Unlike the typical student/teacher friendship, however, we have remained friends ever since.

I have watched Grace grow over the years, academically, from an unmotivated struggling high school student, into a determined, focused, and committed college graduate. More importantly I have watched her grow personally—from a rather self-centered teen into a giving and caring young lady always ready to help those around her.

The proverbial *watershed* for Grace was the tragic death of her long-time best friend shortly after they graduated high school. Already attending community college, I knew in the days that followed the tragedy Grace would do one of two things, become incredibly focused on her education or fall off the edge. Her transcripts and her proud smile at the mention of them will tell you which occurred.

The transcripts, however, only tell part of the story. They won't talk about the two and three jobs at a time Grace held down—even during school—in order to have no student loan debt. They won't tell you about the random visits to her late friend's mother that still continue. They won't reveal the pride in her voice one day a couple of years ago when she called to tell me she had decided to stop smoking pot, completely and for good, nor her response when I asked why: *Because when I looked around at the people I admired the most and most wanted to pattern my life after, people like my mom, some of my professors, and you, pot was not a part of their lives—not one of them.*

The high school and college transcripts will show scholastic growth; they'll tell the best of Grace academically; they won't tell the best of Grace—but I just did.

Yours truly,
Stephen P. MacKenzie, MA Lit.
Department of English, chair

Can you imagine all the stored up memories I wandered through? Can you picture all the smiles they brought? Think about how much pleasure I got from the thirty or forty minutes I got to spend, alone, just remembering all those great things about

Grace.

"Hey, Mr. Mac, would you write me a reference for college?" is how they ask. *Hey, Mr. Mac, would you be willing to spend a half-hour or so remembering the very best about me and writing it down?* is how I hear.

"I'd be honored to" is how I respond.

This column originally appeared in Foster's Daily Democrat, Dover, NH on October 25, 2007.

Feedback: Giving and Getting

I love getting feedback from my students at the end of a course. Yes, in many cases it ends up being a massage-fest, as I tend to get pretty good student reviews. But sometimes the evaluations are really helpful. For example, following my first year at Somersworth High several of my Honors IV evaluations suggested moving both sections of the course into the first semester, since that was the time seniors needed to be gearing up for college applications, final swings at the SATs, etc. We thought that made sense, and Honors English IV has been a semester one course ever since.

Another suggestion was that I change the way I structure the 8-10 page research paper for Honors IV (unless I could scrap it altogether!). Typically, I have a rough draft date for major papers at which time students will peer conference their essays in small groups. Several years ago a number of students suggested that having two rough draft dates, and thus two rounds of peer conferencing, for the larger, more comprehensive research paper would help them avoid falling behind or getting grossly off track with the paper's objectives. Since that time I have scheduled two such dates for the research paper—and it has helped greatly.

Other feedback has demonstrated that our trip to the UNH ropes course is a great way to kick off the class, that my choices of literature are working, and that my major papers are preparing the kids for what will come at the post-secondary level. Of course I also discover, on an almost annual basis, that most of them really dislike writing the research paper and even more dislike dealing with Shakespeare—oh well!

The more recent phenomenon, however, is the source of feedback, for now I am receiving it from the general public, including old friends, new friends, and former students—from San Francisco to Knoxville to Framingham. I've heard from parents and other relatives of students, both current and past. I've received notes, letters, and emails from old classmates, retired colleagues, teachers from neighboring districts, and people I have never met. I've even heard from friends of my parents, both of whom would be almost ninety if they were still living. I received an email from a former student who teaches in Hampton saying how much he loved one of my columns, *All about Charlie*, and had put a copy of it in every teacher's mailbox in his building. I've had feedback from school board members, one of whom suggested I pod-cast the column (which I might do as soon as I learn how), and from a teacher I don't know who was thanking me for "helping the public understand what being a real teacher entails," which is, after all, the reason I started the column in the first place. I had a note from a dad apologizing for not having taught his son the definition of "tithe," and another from someone who could not understand why I would be eating apples in front of my students. Most of those emails and comments send me from my inbox to my smile box, or the Kleenex box, but the note I got today from Lloyd sent me to my bookcase—for a grammar handbook.

Make no mistake this letter was very complimentary of my work but raised a question for which I did not have a ready answer, a question about a phrase from a column which appeared a few weeks ago: ". . . a Robert who goes by Bobby (but who looks just like his older brother John who I had several years ago) . . ." Lloyd wrote that if he had been writing that sentence he'd have been tempted to use "'whom' I had several years ago" as opposed to "'who' I had several years ago." He explained that he believed "the word [the pronoun] is the objective/predicate of the verb 'had' and thus should be 'whom,' the objective case." He closed by saying that the use of *who* or *whom* in these instances had always bothered him and perhaps I could "enlighten him." Hum, I thought, he may be right.

Now I hate taking notes for a group because it embarrasses me when I misspell a word in front of a crowd—I mean I am after all an English teacher—but I love it when someone asks me an English question for which I have to go researching an answer. This time I went scurrying for my Harbrace Handbook of English.

Old Mr. Harbrace, I assume there was once such a person, says this on the subject:

WRONG: *The artist and the model who he loved had a quarrel.*
RIGHT: *The artist and the model whom he loved had a quarrel.* [Whom
    is the object of loved]

<u>he | loved | whom</u>

Lloyd, you are quite correct. In my sentence *whom* is the object of *had* and thus *whom* is the correct pronoun.

<u>I | had | whom</u>

I need to keep a dictionary in my desk and I never *volunteer* to serve as a group scribe. No doubt I'll always have to mentally recite the little "i before e" rhyme when I type *receipt* or *achievement*. There will be no dropping of "Hamlet" or the research paper from my Honors IV syllabus. And I'm sure I will continue to munch my apples, bananas, and grapes in class (you'd be surprised how many of my students claim they find themselves eating more healthy foods after taking my course). But please keep the feedback coming, for who knows how many columns it may generate, and I love it when I learn new things, or even relearn old things. Oh, and

Lloyd, Mr. Harbrace also added that "the relative and interrogative pronouns are especially troublesome," so don't punish yourself too much—and I won't either.

This column originally appeared in Foster's Daily Democrat, Dover, NH on October 11, 2007.

Have Any Suggestions?

I got an email from a fellow English teacher sometime last spring. We had communicated electronically off and on during my annual second semester "sabbatical" through notes, minutes, agenda, short messages, and the like. We had exchanged both information and pleasantries over several weeks. This email was different. It was professional not personal. It was short but loaded. It seemed a simple request, yet I felt concern and frustration hidden in its brevity.

Hi Steve,

I hope you are enjoying the sun!

I was wondering if you had any suggestions on working with either Joe Madden or Janice Brown (not their real names). Joe is doing minimal work outside of school, but I can get him to complete work in the classroom. Janice is new to my class and she mentioned that she was in your class before. Any suggestions on either of these [two]?

I would appreciate any thoughts or ideas you could give me.

Thanks,

(name omitted)

My initial response was a fond "Wow, it's been a while since I thought about those two." Subsequent thoughts were less fond and more critical—of me. One of those students was making a fourth or fifth trip through the same course—several with me as the guide. The other spent more class time in the cafetorium and the nurse's office than in my room. When they came to class they came with nothing—no books, paper, writing utensils, nothing—

every time! Well, almost every time. Once in a while I could get in-class assignments done, but not many. One of them was a good reader and would almost always read when asked; the other would read but only to shut me up. "Have any suggestions," I was asked?

I thought about my classes with Joe and Janice, and whether or not I did have any suggestions. I wasn't sure I did. My experiences had not been very successful, and sometimes they had been downright unpleasant. The last time I had Joe in class he attended most of the time but had produced almost no work. I remember giving back a test one day. He looked at his and said, "A 42! I worked hard on this test. Thanks a lot, friend!" He then tossed it in the trash. I tried to explain, "Joe, when you do almost no work in a unit you can't expect to do well on the test." He didn't hear a word.

Janice was little different except she spent as much time cutting class as she did attending it. She also occasionally had a pen, which usually served as more of a toy—incessant clicking, disassembling/reassembling, draining the ink—than an educational tool. About the only thing Janice would do was read. She was a good reader and a willing one—when she was in class. Hmm, I kept thinking, do I have any suggestions?

Well, I replied to the email but I'm sure it wasn't too useful. I admitted that while I knew these two kids loved me, and I them, that had not translated into them achieving much in my class. I said that Joe would sometimes do classroom work, he especially liked poetry, but he virtually never did homework. I said I thought part of him wanted to be successful but only on his terms. I was able to say that for the most part he was respectful.

About Janice I said that sadly she just seemed to be a lost soul. I suspected home support was minimal and that though I knew she liked me—told me all the time—she accomplished almost nothing in my class. I did add that she was one of my best readers and that might be something on which to capitalize.

I knew it wasn't a lot but I thought it was the best I could do. It must have read like *here's my experience, don't expect much, good luck.* But I didn't stop thinking about my colleague or Joe and Janice after clicking "send." Joe was being raised, along with at least two other siblings, by a single working mom, with no father actively involved, to the best of my knowledge. Janice was at least as much trouble to her mom as she was to us. I think we were actually happy when she moved away from Somersworth, a move we thought was permanent. Why didn't I *know* whether or not there was a dad in Joe's life? Why didn't I do more to encourage his poetry? Why didn't I play more to Janice's reading and spelling abilities? Why didn't I know more about her home life? What if her mother was as glad to have her move away as we were! One less problem, right?

No, that reply wasn't the best I could have done, not even close. I'd send a very different reply today, because if I had another chance with those students I'd be a very different teacher. I'd focus more on *their* need to achieve than my own. I'd try to be more helpful with the things that frustrate their lives (and thus inhibit their education) and worry less about how they frustrated mine. If I had another chance I'd go back to that email, hit "reply" and write . . .

Dear Colleague,
I don't know if I can be helpful or not but I'll try. Clearly both of these folks have forces at work outside of school, which inhibit their success in school. See if you can find out what they are and how you can help. After that, build on Janice's strong reading skills and Joe's love of poetry (even if it is only to impress his girlfriend!) And if none of that works just love them, every day,

even more than I did. It may not translate into good grades but a lost grade is preferable to a lost soul.

Stay in touch,

Steve

This column originally appeared in Foster's Daily Democrat, Dover, NH on April 10, 2007.

150 Years Later

What do you say to your colleagues when they retire? Good luck on the golf course? Happy rocking? I'm pea green with envy? You look pretty good for your age? What? I know how I got into this thought process—it happened when I printed off the flyer Jan sent out from the front office announcing the party for this year's high school retirees to be held on May 29. The headline virtually shouted "It's Time for a Hilltopper RETIREMENT CELEBRATION!"

My boss's name was there, a fellow English teacher who has been my next-door-neighbor for the last eleven school years, a colleague in the Career Technical Center who is also a thirty plus year personal friend, and several others. Anyway, I got to thinking, as I went down the list, of all the knowledge and experience those people represented.

Brian has spent ten years at the helm of Somersworth High. He guided us through our last NEASC accreditation process, has sought out and instituted new ways to celebrate students and their accomplishments, both gifted and struggling students. In ten years I have never gone to him with a request that would benefit my students that he has not found a way to grant: bus funds for a field trip, a new set of books, help with a parent, or permission to go to a suspended student's house to give a test. Together we've done late night interviews, suffered through insufferable meetings, attended Top Ten breakfasts, and cheered our sports teams. Of course I did have to teach him that you start the coffee maker with cold water not hot, but it's all good!

Next was Sheila, a member of our guidance department for almost three decades. I have listened to more seniors complain about how she pushed them to get their college information to her, but they sure liked getting their applications done. I have worked with her on one of our student support teams, experiencing first-hand how dedicated she is to our students. I have seen many times how caring, gentle and supportive she is with some of our most vulnerable.

Then came Minnett. Minnett and I have been colleagues for the last eleven years, but we have been friends for more than thirty. She has dedicated much of her life to administering vocational assessments, organizing and hosting job fairs, and counseling. We have worked together to help several students graduate or make it through their English class. For two years when we were short staffed she even taught a section of freshmen English. She had been out of the formal classroom for many years but you'd never have known it!

When I was nineteen years old my lifetime next-door-neighbors in Rollinsford moved to Virginia. It was strange not to have them on the other end of the path that connected our two house lots. It will be strange not having Nick as my next-door-neighbor at school next year. Nick and I never shared Tonka Trucks, cookouts, or summertime glasses of Tang, but we have shared student work, classroom experiences, jokes, and books. I remember commiserating with him one time early in my career and he looked at me and said, "Well, I'd like to think I've gotten better over the years, but you know, Steve, my first year teaching . . . I was so bad I should have had to pay them!" Hum, I thought, maybe there is hope for me.

Next on the list was Jean, who runs the Early Childhood Education program in the Career Tech Center. Now mind you Jeanie's room is located in the opposite corner of the building from my room, so we don't cross paths a lot, but that doesn't mean I haven't experienced her skills and learned from her. I loved the occasional trips I would make to her classroom and see our students in action with the little ones. I always looked forward to having the Topper Tots come into my classroom in full costume during their annual Halloween Parade through the high school! Many of my students have also had Early Childhood Ed and loved it, and Jean. And more than a few graduated with plans for careers in nursery school or day care.

Finally I came to Carol's name, our assistant librarian for some twenty years. What amazes me most about Carol is that I have never seen her show even the slightest hint of anger, frustration, or irritation at school. She is perhaps the most even tempered staff person in the building. She is gentle and soft-spoken. I've never heard her yell. I've never even heard her raise her voice. For twenty years she has come into the building on a daily basis with her calm, placid demeanor just quietly going about helping kids locate the materials they need, cataloging newspapers and books, assisting teachers, and generally helping to make our school run more efficiently.

OK, Steve, so what's the point? Well the point is I'm serving as the emcee for their retirement celebration tonight. I want to say something about them, about all they have brought to our school and to the lives of their students and colleagues. Of course I may tell Carol that an occasional yell can be rather cleansing. And I really ought to let Jeanie know what I think about her Topper Tots having to build "snowpeople" instead of snowmen! I'll probably let Brian know that I doubt I'll have to teach the next principal how to make coffee! But here's what I really want to say to these friends and colleagues who will depart having served us for nearly a century and a half. "Thank you for all the money you'll save us in the next year's salaries and benefits budget! I'm just kidding! Truthfully, everything I've said so far was just a long preface to this: I hope you have some sense of how your career has positively impacted so many lives. Somersworth High School and Career Technical Center is a better place because of you. I love you. I honor you. And multiplied out over 150 years, I'm only one of thousands!"

This column originally appeared in Foster's Daily Democrat, Dover, NH on June 3, 2008.

The New Principal

There will be a lot of changes at Somersworth High this year. Some teachers left to pursue new careers, a few switched departments, and several retired, all of which resulted in a number of moves and new hires. None of the changes, however, will have more impact on the life of Somersworth High than the retirement of Brian Flanagan, our principal for the last ten years. Our new principal, Mrs. Sharon Lampros, officially began her duties on July 1st. Mrs. Lampros has a long (*to wit*, it took her weeks to move out of her classroom!) and successful history at Somersworth High and enjoys great respect among the faculty and staff. Having dedicated some thirty-plus years of her life to Somersworth, as a math teacher and then assistant principal, it seems fitting that I share with you (and with her) some of my thoughts about this most dedicated educator.

Dear Sharon,

Forgive me for the very public setting of this rather personal letter, but I could think of no better nor more fitting a venue for conveying the thoughts I wish to share. There are many of us out here, directly and indirectly connected to Somersworth High, who are not only pleased but excited that you are our new principal, and I want all of the seacoast to know it.

You will recall we began working together in the fall of 1997 when I joined the SHS English department and we became "neighbors." You were the person I went to when I didn't know who else to go to. You answered my questions about the daily schedule, the calendar, and where to get supplies. When I needed a mentor for my Alternative 5 certification program you agreed to help. During those first months when I was spending almost every minute of every day in my room teaching, prepping, or stressing you were the one who said, "Steve, as necessary as time in the classroom is, it's also important that you get out of it some and build relationships with your colleagues. Why don't you start by coming down to the teacher's room once in a while for lunch?"

You had the extra pads of attendance slips when I ran out, the words of advice when I had questions about a student, the proper "delayed opening" or "early dismissal" schedules when I forgot about them, and the much needed hugs when my mother died. Along with your shoulder I have borrowed 3x5 cards, pencils, paper, your rolling cart, markers, masking tape, and yardsticks. I have no idea how you ever found those things in your very "lived in" classroom, but you always did!

By my second and third year our relationship became a bit less one-sided. We helped each other through the learning pains of a computerized program for grading and attendance. Along with some of our other friends we made shared fools of ourselves on stage at *two* school assemblies with our dance and lip-sync rendition of "We Are Family." We nearly drove ourselves nuts learning the Measures in Academic Progress testing system, and closer to insanity as we began the process of developing our course competencies two years ago. We have worked through accreditation, helped hire a new superintendent, and sponsored bi-weekly social hours for new faculty members. We've attended workshops, meetings, forums, and conferences. You helped get me certified and I helped you draft word problems and rubrics. You're into parallel lines and challenges; I'm into parallel structures and chocolate—remember those Funny Bones and Ring Dings I used to bring you at the beginning of block four? Of course, that was *before* the superintendent made the cafeteria people go all healthy!

Over a year ago when you applied for the assistant principal position you asked me for a letter of reference. In it I wrote,

> "Yes, there are any number of ways in which Sharon Lampros, by virtue of her intellectual prowess and wide-reaching leadership experience, would add significantly to the administration of Somersworth High School, and in many ways has been doing just that for years. But there is also the Sharon Lampros who rarely leaves school before 4:00 in the afternoon, sometimes 5:00, working with students who need extra help; the Sharon Lampros who was devastated at the death of Sonny Sip and who helped hold me up when Adam Routhier died, checking on me regularly for days. That's the Sharon Lampros I want to be sure you know, the one with whom I am privileged to serve the students and parents of Somersworth High School. Will I miss her across the hall? You bet. But I will be assured of the intelligence and dedication she will bring to the front office, and absolutely certain that policy, personnel, and disciplinary decisions will be made with integrity, and implemented with concern for all."

I meant every word of that then, and I still mean it now. I have been very proud to be your colleague and I am equally proud to be a part of your faculty. More than that, though, I am honored to be your friend. No, I'm not across the hall from you anymore, but I'm only a "buzz" or email away. I will still pop in for a start-of-the-day hug, I will still proofread anything you'd like, and I *always* have a box of Famous Amos chocolate chip cookies in my room. I know we're going to have a great year.

Love,
Steve

Now, it might appear to the casual reader that I am attempting to suck up to my new boss in a big way. Not true—believe me. When I screw up, Sharon will let me know it—kindly and with dignity, but directly. When Sharon's new office gets a bit too "lived in," I'll let her know it—somehow. And when things go right, we'll let each other know it. After all, We Are Family, on stage and off.

This column originally appeared in Foster's Daily Democrat, Dover, NH on July 22, 2008.

Response and Responsibility

A few weeks ago, as part of my *War on Trial* unit, which features Elie Wiesel's book *Night* as well as the movie Schindler's List, one of my colleagues and I took a group of our seniors to Washington, D.C. We saw the Vietnam Veterans Memorial, the WWII Memorial, the Lincoln Memorial, the White House, the Capitol Building, and some of the Smithsonian. The larger purpose of the field trip, however, was to see the United States Holocaust Museum. I wanted my students to *experience* in some small way what they had read and watched on video.

I recognize that it's not possible to really experience the Holocaust through a museum, but we did come away with a better, more visual understanding of what Elie Weisel and others like him experienced during those horrible years of Auschwitz, Dachau, and the other death camps. We were able to see the faces, hear the words, watch the pain of some of those who survived— and the many who did not.

As a final assessment to this unit I assigned a five-paragraph essay on a prompt I wrote based on some of Wiesel's final words of the Preface to his new translation of *Night*. In the last paragraphs of that Preface we read,

Sometimes I am asked if I know "the response to Auschwitz"; I answer that not only do I not know it, but that I don't even know if a tragedy of this magnitude has a response. What I do know is that there is "response" in responsibility. When we speak of this era of evil and darkness, so close and yet so distant, "responsibility" is the key word.

The witness has forced himself to testify. For the youth of today, for

the children who will be born tomorrow. He does not want his past to become their future.

—Elie Wiesel

My final question to my students was, "what is *your* response to Auschwitz, *Night*, and all that they represent?" I want to share with you excerpts of some of their answers:

A pebble tossed into a river causes a ripple effect that touches the shores and everything between them. The Holocaust symbolizes a boulder cast into the stream of history. Its impact was detrimental to its decade, and its waves are still surging upon us today . . . To visualize Night *leaves me shocked and frightened. Often times I am afraid to try. Self control eludes me at seeing the "truck draw close and unload its hold; small children. Babies . . . thrown into the flames." Scars run deep where this image is preserved.*

—Craig R

When I read this book, every page at least once moved me to tears. I am now so thankful, having been educated about the Holocaust, that I have the life I do. "Never shall I forget the nocturnal silence that deprived me for all eternity of the desire to live." Never shall I forget Night.

—Emily S

My response to Night, Auschwitz *and all it represents is simple: I will not forget those who died. I cannot. For if I do their legacy, their death is in vain . . . I should not be comfortable if someone is hungry, thirsty, imprisoned without reason, violated. As a citizen of this world, I will do my best to accept the responsibility of never forgetting that* Night.

—Becky E

Subjected to a world of disparity, torture, and hatred what is to be expected of faith; faith in God, faith in destiny, other than to go up in smoke with the ashes of the victims of the crematoria. The atrocious actions of evil men resulted in the unveiling of a truth we would have all preferred be left to mystery: the limits of faith.

—Alex R

"And as the train stopped, this time we saw flames rising from a tall chimney into a black sky." This was just the beginning of the terror that I felt reading [Night]. All I could see while reading was what they saw: ashes of loved ones roaming throughout the sky. All I could feel is what they felt: agony, frightened, worried, anger. All I could do is what they did: cry.

—Danielle S

The response is one I just can't find a word for. Emotion is what hits me the most. After witnessing the very shoes which the Jews would wear at these camps, hundreds and hundreds of pairs, just made me depressed. Knowing a young boy put his own two feet in them at one time. The very age of me, robbed of his life, the chance of having a family, the chance of growing up. It's just indescribable; so much so I can't even comprehend what I'm thinking right now because the picture is still fresh in my mind.

—Albert B

One of my students, Thay Costa, a foreign exchange student, offered a somewhat different answer in the form of a rather powerful analogy. She wrote that "responsibility is a reaction." She went on to say that many world leaders in the 30s and 40s "didn't do their job because they had in their hands [the ability] to save those lives, but decided just to wash their hands [of the Jews] in the same way as Pontius Pilate did with Jesus."

Like Wiesel, I don't know if there really is a response to Auschwitz and the Holocaust as a whole. I still don't know, even after having lived some fifty-one years, how it could have happened, how the world could have *let* it happen. But I do know forty-six seniors at Somersworth High School whose lives, in some ways, were forever changed because of Wiesel's story. I can't tell you exactly what that change will look like or what they will do because of it. But I know this; they won't wash their hands of it.

This column originally appeared in Foster's Daily Democrat, Dover, NH on December 2, 2008.

Making My Day

I have to tell you, yesterday did not start off great. First of all I was at school at 7:45 AM. Now that might not seem too bad as I'm usually getting there by 5:45 AM, but this was a Saturday! Yes, I can grade at home and do—frequently. But the end of the semester, and thus my classes, is coming up fast, which means all the make-up work, last minute rewrites, and final assignments have come in and the pile is pretty high. And while I can grade at home I can't enter the grades into GradeQuick from home. Besides, I tend to stay focused better when there is no phone, personal computer, TV, or endless supply of coffee to distract me. So to school I went with a goal of making a serious dent in the backed up work—particularly in the last set of papers from my seniors.

I did remember to stop at Cumby's and get my chocolate raspberry coffee, so all was not horrible as I sat down at my desk and started reading forty-six critical papers. Fortunately, the papers were not horrible either and, amazingly, every single student had turned one in—on time! The problem was, though far from horrible, a lot of them were not all that great either, which always causes me to worry that I didn't do a very good job teaching how to write whatever it is I'm reading, in this case literary criticism.

The thing with literary criticism is that it's not an easy concept for a lot of high school students to grasp. Frequently, kids don't even encounter criticism until college, but I like my students to have some minor experience with criticism/analysis before they leave my room. The tough part for most of them is trying to avoid two traps, plot summary and reader response. Literary criticism is analyzing a piece of literature through a particular lens, or with a specific bias if you'd rather. In other words you need to have formulated some *idea* about this piece of writing or its author. For example, let's say I wanted to write a critical paper on *Great Expectations*. My thesis statement might read something like "Even with its rather formal, perhaps cumbersome, maybe even antiquated language, Dickens is still engaging audiences and inciting *great expectations*, even in today's twenty-first century." Or if I wanted to write on some of the works of Stephen King, I might draft a statement like "It may well be that King's fiction, fantasy, and sci-fi greater explore the depths of real-life and real-world issues than do many works of nonfiction." The point is, you can't have a successful piece of criticism without a thesis statement. I don't want you to tell me *what* happened because I already know that. And I don't want to know how the piece you're criticizing makes you *feel* because, for this assignment, I don't care about that. I want to know more of the "hows" and "whys" in this paper.

So I had read my way through several different accounts of what happened to Elie Wiesel, as if I didn't know, and a number of different ways in which students related to or reacted to *Tuesdays with Morrie*, as if I cared (actually, I do, very much, but not for this paper). Then I got to Laura's paper. Like quite a few others, Laura had written on Weisel's *Night*. Unlike several of her peer's, however, she didn't get stuck on her reactions to or feelings about the atrocities of the Holocaust (an easy thing to do), or how she could never have survived the camps as Wiesel did. No, Laura's paper, "Surviving Without Faith," had a thesis, a clear, strong thesis: "During the Holocaust is when you would think you would need your God most, but Wiesel and other victims thought otherwise, and in a way [denying God] helped them [by giving] them more strength to fight." Oh yes! My day just got so much better. A really good paper! Maybe I could have taught the lesson better but at least I didn't totally blow it. Not only did the lead have a thesis but she spent the body of the paper discussing and defending that thesis—just like she was supposed to do.

I got so excited I called Laura when I got done grading her paper to tell her what a good job she'd done. Suddenly my mountain of papers seemed much more manageable. I actually got an entire class finished by the time my coffee was gone, and I left the building feeling pretty good—not knowing I was destined to feel even better.

When I got home a couple of hours later I had received an email from Laura's mom, which said in part, "I was home when Laura got your call about her paper and I want you to know that you play a huge role in your students' lives. Having not done so well in pre calc, hearing [good news] from you at this time meant a great deal to her. [As I'm sure you know] Laura doesn't sugar coat anything . . . It's a great quality to have, unless you are in high school. She stood alone for a long time and your class, allowing [your students] to speak from their hearts, has really helped her to open up. People misjudge way too often in this world and I just want to thank you for impacting [Laura] in a positive way."

I'm betting you can guess what that did for a day that started out being a Saturday morning at school, with piles of backed up work. That simple phone call made Laura's day, and her mom's email made mine. Shoot I'll bet I could take on another set or two of papers . . . but not today.

This column originally appeared in Foster's Daily Democrat, Dover, NH on January 27, m2009.

I Have to Tell You

Listen, if you're a parent and you don't get to parent conferences, whenever your school has them, you're making a big mistake—if you can possibly make it—and if you can't you should schedule some other time to come in and meet with your kid's teachers. You need to hear what's going on in your kid's life while he or she is at school, and you need to hear it from their teachers. Now if you've got a daughter or son at Somersworth High, you have that opportunity this coming Thursday when we host Parent Conferences. So you should come here on March 12th at 6:00 pm. No, really, you *need* to come because I want to talk to you, and so does every other teacher in the building, at least they should. *Why?* you might ask. Because we have very important things to tell you and to discuss with you and to share with you.

Some days, most days frankly, the coolest things happen in my classroom. Sometimes they just involve me, other times they involve everybody. Take the other day. I actually had a student bring me in a huge bowl of beef stew that his mom had made. The day before that I learned how to greet someone in Indonesian: *apa kabar*. And another day that week a student shared with us some of the differences between traditional Egyptian concepts of the extended "family" and the more modern western concept of the nuclear family. We also learned that today, even in Egypt, technology and gadgetry are slowly supplanting "family time" with family "stuff." Things like that happen almost every day in my classroom.

Other things happen, too, that are every bit as cool. I was working one on one for a few minutes the other day with a student who really struggles with reading—particularly reading aloud. I think he read *six sentences* out loud to me as we worked to figure out which ones were complete sentences and which were not. How cool is that? Then there was last Wednesday, when my question of the day was, *share with us, please, something you fear.* Well, we had the usual run of *heights, spiders, snakes, death, cancer,* etc. But one student shared, "I fear being rejected, because it happens a lot." And the next person said, "I fear other people's opinions of me." After pausing a couple of seconds I turned to the rest of the class and said, "You guys, do you realize the compliment they paid you? They didn't just answer the question, they also said, "I trust you to have this information, to know this about me." What an honor!

It's not just my classroom where these things occur either; it's every classroom in the building at one time or another. You should see the roller coasters that get built in some of the science classes and the bridges that get made out of spaghetti in some of the math classes. For their contribution to our fall Renaissance Fair, Jackie's class was making posters on various assigned topics associated with the era. One student created this tri-fold poster on Shakespeare that boasted a multi-modal presentation of the bard's life: personal statistics, his writings, his contributions to the world of literature. It was outstanding!

I was moaning one day recently to Jim Niland, our auto mechanics teacher, about the stupid "check engine" light that had been on in my truck for months, maybe years, and that I kept forgetting to have my mechanic check it out. He told me to bring it in the next day. He had a student plug a handheld computer into a port under my dash. I didn't even know the port was there (nor did I know we had such a computer) but in about three minutes the kid knew what was wrong and how to fix it!

Are you getting it? All you moms, dads, stepparents, guardians, do you see how we need you? I know, sometimes we also need to talk with you about a behavior issue or some missing homework or a paper that's late. We can't always avoid a negative or two, but there are so many more important things we need to tell you. Like I need to tell one parent how worried I was about having his son in class, since I'd once had a rather unpleasant encounter with him while covering for a colleague. But he has grown up so much and has actually become one of my class's "go to" kids this year. I need to tell another parent that her son beat me at push ups—not an easy thing to do (though I do think he bent the rules a bit!). There's another parent that I absolutely have to tell how hard his daughter is working to overcome her fear of reading aloud in class, and still others who *have* to hear how much their son is trying to manage his anger more successfully. All these things, and many more, we have to tell you about your kids.

So you see, you need to come. Yes, you may hear about something that's not pleasing. Maybe a grade that's hurting, or that it would help if you could reinforce the necessity of homework. But I can tell you this; in my room you're going to hear way more positives about your kid than negatives. You may hear that your child is proudly developing trust in their classmates and in me. You may hear me talk about how much your child contributes to our classroom experiences by their sharing of differences in cultural and linguistic traditions. I may say to you, *apa kabar*, or you may hear me compliment you on your beef stew. Whatever it is I need you to come, because I have to tell you.

This column originally appeared in Foster's Daily Democrat, Dover, NH on March 10, 2009.

PART VI

...ETC.

Some things are fairly easy to categorize, other things, not so much. Literature, for example, can often be grouped or categorized according to theme, or era, or topic. Same kind of thing for writing—fiction or nonfiction, sometimes author. Food, beverages can also be easily categorized in most cases, as can automobiles, clothing, houses, and the list can go on. This next section of columns (or articles, as many of my readers called them) didn't easily fit into a category, hence the " . . . etc." They're just kind of random, a potpourri, if you will, of thoughts and ideas and topics. While you're reading, if you come up with an idea for a category under which I should have placed them, please share your feedback with me.

Sticking Around

There is something to be said for growing up and moving away. You can build a new life without a lot of baggage. No one has preconceived notions about you based on past experiences. You get to "start fresh," try new things, meet new people, and make new friendships. You could join a new church, buy a car without your dad's help or influence, maybe even vote for a Democrat (although, I think my dad had passed away before the time I voted for Jeanne Shaheen for governor). Anyway, there is a lot to be said for taking off to parts unknown.

There's also a lot to be said, however, for sticking around home and letting your roots grow even deeper (to use a really bad cliché that I would never allow in a student paper). My feet walked the same halls of Rollinsford Grade School as did many of my students'. I, too, attended Somersworth Middle School—during its early years of the very modern "open concept"! My bike rode the same streets theirs do minus a few subdivisions that didn't exist thirty-five or forty years ago. I had the Wilson boys in class. I went to school with their dad, and their mom is chair of the Rollinsford School Board. I like that. I like it that one of the past Rollinsford chairpersons, Jay Hanson, was a childhood friend, that he and his family have always attended the same church I do, and that his son took three different classes with me. I like it that Paula, our teachers association president, who is also one of my closest colleagues, attended my mother's kindergarten—we even lived on the same street growing up.

I also have any number of connections to students at Somersworth High. I was friends and/or classmates with several of Taryn's aunts and uncles on the Bertrand side. I had the granddaughter of my father's best man in class. A couple of years ago I asked a young lady who took up residence outside my door each morning what her name was.

"Jessica," she replied.

"Jessica what?" I pursued.

"Jessica Randall."

"Hum, any relation to the Randalls over near Crockett's Crossing."

"Yes!" she responded brightly, that's my family."

"So let's see—if you're a Randall then you must have an Aunt Lynne, right?'

"I sure do. She's my father's sister."

"Yeah, so is Earl your father or your Uncle?"

"He's my Uncle."

"OK, he was a little ahead of me I think, but I'm pretty sure I was in the same class as your aunt."

See, I like being able to make those connections. It's not like I couldn't have made it in Duluth, or Dubuque, or Dubrovnik for that matter; but having longevity in a place—it's nice.

Take Minnett for example, a member of our guidance department and the Career Technical Center: I met Minnett in the mid 70's when her family joined my church. I used to walk through the white elephant room of our church fair with her daughters—Maria on one arm and Natalie on the other. But it was Maria I could bait.

"Maria," I would start, "wouldn't you like mommy to buy you this?" as I picked up some previously used toy or trinket.

"Mommy, will you buy me this?"

"Oh and Maria! wouldn't you like mommy to buy you this?" holding up some equally unnecessary thing," all the while Minnett trying to thwart my efforts!

I must admit, I cost her some money (I was very persuasive and Maria was very stubborn!), but it was all in good fun, and it supported our church.

Yet the story doesn't stop there. Somehow between Minnett and me we managed to get Pete through high school. Having dual certification, several years back she filled in twice in my department to teach a section of English I, because we were very short staffed at the time. It was there that she met a student named John, a student I also came to know and have in class. Two years later we would have that link when we both ended up at his house to support him after his dad died as a result of a tragic accident. We were able to be supportive to him—and to each other—in large part because of our long history together. I've lost count of how many times we have conferenced with, celebrated with, and occasionally agonized with each other over one student or another, always searching for how we could best serve that student.

Could I have moved away or commuted to another district? Sure I could have. Would I have had a successful career? I'd like to think so. But Paula and I would not be able to lighten the mood during contract negotiations, or meetings about the latest school initiative, with stories of her parents or mine, and Mrs. MacKenzie's Kindergarten. I couldn't reminisce with kids about summer bike rides on their street, unless they live in one of those subdivisions that used to be a cornfield, hayfield, or woods. I wouldn't be able to mention places like Scout Land or Crockett's Crossing with the certainty that many of my students know those places. It wouldn't mean anything when I talk about swimming in Hanson's pond when I was a kid, or biking on Baer Road over to Old Mill Lane via a long-ago closed road and a really scary (and incredibly unsafe!) bridge. There would be no understanding of the dump-turned-transfer station, or the school annex, or the open concept middle school which has been walled for decades now—thank goodness.

I'm glad I chose to stick around. Yes, I know nothing lasts forever. For instance, Minnett is retiring this year and her daughters are all grown up. But we still attend St. John's, there's still a white elephant room at the fair . . . and she has grandchildren!

*Some names have been changed in "Sticking Around."

This column originally appeared in Foster's Daily Democrat, Dover, NH on March 13, 2008.

Another Year Over and Deeper in Debt

I say it every year: I have no idea where the first semester went. It feels like a few weeks ago I was passing out syllabi, distributing textbooks, and listening to students complain about the heat. Since then we have swung from trees at UNH's ropes course, worked with texts such as the Book of Ruth from the Bible, Tim O'Brien's *The Things They Carried*, O. Henry's "The Gift of the Magi," Elie Wiesel's *Night*, Stockton's "The Lady, or the Tiger?" Bambara's "My Delicate Heart Condition," and many others. We've written personal narratives, persuasive papers, and research papers. We've discussed literature, politics, religion, families, marriage, money, war, forgiveness, and love. We've touched on real estate values, and family values, and value added taxes. We have laughed, cried, stressed, complimented, supplemented, and experimented. I had motivated students, "whatever" students, and whiners. Interestingly enough, the guy who whined the most about his eight to ten page research paper—he conferenced it with me at least three times, each time complaining more vehemently than the last that he could not possible get three, then two, then one more page—ended up getting the highest grade in the class.

Yup, it's been quite a semester—and not just because of the whiners either. No it's been quite a semester for a lot of reasons. One is, I feel like I haven't stopped grading papers and homework since early September—because I haven't. My last pile, unless someone brings me in a late paper on Monday, is down on my kitchen table. Additionally, I'm not sure I fully appreciated just how much work my kids actually did this year. When I was reading over my freshmen final exam, for example, I couldn't believe how many different things I had to assess. There was a section on vocabulary and one on our short story unit, another on nonfiction, another on grammar, another on literary terms (twenty of them!), and yet another on poetry. We also had a section on Romeo and Juliet, one on *Of Mice and Men*, and the last section involved reading a new short story and answering ten comprehension questions. It really was quite an exam—thank God my wife is helping me grade the objective sections! And lastly, the only way I got any exercising in was by going into the high school weight room three mornings a week at 5:30. That means I got even less sleep than normal and normal is none too much.

Then there were my seniors. I don't know how many hours I have into reading, commenting on, and grading their papers, but way over a hundred. I also spent hours and hours keeping up with the homework readings I assigned (it's hard to facilitate a good discussion if you're not fresh on what happened, not to mention I always find something I missed the first eight or ten times I've read something). And then outside of class I have several dozen hours into writing teacher references and letters of recommendation and conferencing college essays. And there's the other dozens I've spent attending games, concerts, plays, and meets. Seriously, I'm exhausted! Now who's whining? But, really, sometimes I wonder how the kids survive.

Still, it's so worth it. Take my seniors' final presentations, for instance. The project's guiding principle was to demonstrate how you have grown as a student during the semester. Many students talked about things like improved writing skills, a new appreciation for literature and reading, and less fear about public speaking. But almost everyone talked about how much closer they felt to their classmates, about how less afraid they were to share their thoughts and ideas and feelings, and about the value and support and love they had felt. See we didn't just learn the traditional stuff, like "show-don't-tell," the engaging lead, the successful conclusion that refers back, or details, details, details in writing good personal narratives. We didn't stop with learning proper MLA formatting and documentation for our research papers, or identifying independent and dependent clauses in our grammar exercises, or connotative versus denotative definitions in our vocabulary lessons. We weren't satisfied to just read aloud and critique a text or answer a few questions. No, we went way beyond simply reading and writing and analyzing—we went to life, our lives.

We didn't just learn that Chris could construct a decent essay; we learned how a fifteen-year-old guy managed to cope with the death of his dad. We learned how devoted Danny is to his brother—not just, but especially, when the difficulties are great. We learned that while she is still a bit quiet and shy, after three years of drifting among several high schools Kim finally feels like she has a home. We learned that Bobby and Devin both dream of being professional athletes, and that even as a Latter Day Saint Amber doesn't really want Mitt Romney to be president . . . because she's not sure she's ready to have Mormons dumped on for the next four years. Through our learning I became part of their lives, but more importantly they became part of mine. That, you see, is why my debt grows so much each year—my debt of thanks for all the ways in which they enrich my life. Oh yes, the time in the classroom, the ridiculously early workouts, the hours of grading, the time spent at extra-curricular activities, it's tough, but it's all worth it. On top of everything I've said we studied and learned, I got to cheer in the stands as Bobby ripped down rebounds. I got to applaud Heather's performance on stage, and shed a tear while I talked to Chris about *my* dad's death.

Shoot, I even noticed a bicep muscle while I was shaving the other morning. The debt? I hope it bankrupts me—what a way to go!

This column originally appeared in Foster's Daily Democrat, Dover, NH on January 29, 2008.

It's Not About Me

A lesson I am continually learning has little to do with academia but everything to do with students and teaching. It's not all about me. I cannot fix all their errors, I did not cause all their troubles, and I am not responsible for all their problems.

I am not a god of grammar and construction, I can't ignore plagiarism, I don't understand how a fifteen-year-old manages to stay home and smoke pot all day, how a sixteen-year-old "got kicked out of [their] house," and I can't explain the meaning of life.

Even in the classroom it's not all about me. I don't understand how a freshman could miss fifteen plus days of school in the first quarter; I don't know how someone who has difficulty constructing a reasonable complex sentence, or who doesn't understand the concept of subject/verb agreement, can end up in Honors English IV. I don't understand how one of my strongest students failed English I last semester. I don't know what any of these things were about, but I know they were not about me.

My most recent "lesson" in this ongoing learning process happened a few weeks ago.

We were discussing Mitch Albom's *Tuesdays With Morrie* and Matt, whose blank face and straining eyes were indicating he was not having a good day, made a statement I thought deserved some questioning.

I said, "Gee, I'm not sure I would agree with that. What about . . ."

"I don't really care if you agree," he interjected.

"Excuse me?" I responded, thinking, Wow! Where did that

come from?

"I don't really care what you agree with. You're always disagreeing with us."

"You know Matt, that was really rude—you can challenge me but you don't have to be rude."

We traded a few more verbal quips and I thought about tossing him, but we simply ended with a "whatever" standoff. Still, all the while I was wondering, *what is going on here?* I know he's had some run-ins with other teachers but I thought he liked me, or at least respected me. Why would he act this way? I don't get it!

A few weeks later I assigned a one page response to random Dali Lama quotes. Matt's quote was "spend some time alone each day." This is what he wrote:

If anyone knows a thing or two about alone time, it's me. Since infancy I have had insomnia. I don't mean this figuratively, I mean staying up for two to three days of sleeplessness. One may wonder what happens to someone after such an extended period of sleep deprivation. Well let me tell you that it involves a lot of "me" time.

As all of my friends head off to bed and the list of people I'm instant messaging with dwindles down, I slowly become isolated. At first I didn't use this time beneficially. I would sit in bed, stare at the clock, and count down the hours until I was to begin the next day. Midnight rolls around, six hours until I have to wake up . . . three in the morning, three more hours. I hated clocks, in fact I still do. They were my enemy with how they would tell me when I should have been sleeping, and then show me all of the time I missed out on sleep. My mind raced as I lay there. Random thoughts would pop into my mind, and I would think about every one of them through and through.

The hard part was picking out useful things; at times my mind would get so cluttered with thoughts that I didn't know what I was thinking about. I just knew I was thinking. It drove me crazy, almost literally. I would bounce between depression and anger; never happiness. It was hard to harness all of the time I had while awake. This is where I developed my curiosity and desire to teach myself. I learned to play bass guitar, I read nearly the entire www.howstuffworks.com website, and I would write journals during times of depression. Later on I'd read these entries and struggle to understand why I was thinking the way I did. It was as if I wasn't me. Someone else was typing, something was sitting on my reason sowing seeds of irrational thoughts.

I wrote about anything that came to mind, be it love, politics, how the mechanics of happy meal toys work, or what it would be like to fly.

For some reason I seemed to absorb everything I learned at night while I was in the altered mind. I wasn't sure why but when I wasn't rotating emotions, I was pleased with my productivity. Unfortunately, one of my biggest burdens was all of this learning and no application. It's not like I had anyone to talk to at four in the morning while I was reading about how special relativity works. This led me to develop the habit of shouting out stupid facts that no one really cares about . . . heck, I didn't even know why I cared about them. I guess I just felt crazy.

See, time spent alone was good when I made it useful. I learned to teach myself something—anything. I learned academics, spirituality, and ultimately things about myself. One of the most important things I learned about myself was that I love learning on my own accord . . . without being told to, and without needing a grade. But you should always remember to get some sleep. Don't ever take it for granted, because the minute you do you might find yourself feeling a little crazy.

—Matt L

The more I read the more I understood, and the happier I was I hadn't tossed him that day. There was an answer, had been all along, and it didn't have a thing to do with me.

This column originally appeared in Foster's Daily Democrat, Dover, NH on February 14, 2008.

On Talking

I don't know too many teachers who don't dread having to constantly speak to their students about talking during class—when they're not supposed to be talking that is. I had a class once where I averaged twenty-plus requests per day: *please stop talking; please be quiet; will you please stop talking.* It got ridiculous. One day a student actually counted my requests—forty-plus as I recall! Yet it was a class that responded well to the curriculum in both reading and writing—go figure.

Still, incessant talking does get incredibly annoying. Sometimes they're talking about what's going on in class, but more typically they're talking about what happened the day before, the class before, or the boyfriend/girlfriend before. They talk about ball games, clothes, hairstyles, cars, lack of money, having to work, college essays, parents, siblings, and food. It doesn't really matter as long as they're talking.

Well, speaking of talking, I have a confession to make . . . and I don't make them easily, not even in private, never mind to possibly thirty or forty thousand Foster's readers. It was December 19, 2007, three days before Christmas vacation. My seniors were in a unit called *Peace with Justice.* We had finished working with Simon Wiesenthal's *The Sunflower* and Martin Luther King's *I have a Dream* speech and moved on to the Dali Lama. This particular day we were also examining some quotes I had pulled off the Web which specifically dealt with ideas of peace. One of those that especially intrigued me was "Greatness comes when we talk." I put it up on the whiteboard and we *talked* about it.

We ended up having some excellent conversations about that

quote and several others, and before I knew it, as is often the case, block one was over. Block two also came and went quickly. In no time my freshmen were coming through the door and . . . and all of a sudden (here comes my confession) it hit me that I had no idea what we were going to do for ninety minutes. We would spend some of the time reviewing for the next day's retest of Steinbeck's *Of Mice and Men*, but that would take no more than half the block, and on Friday, after the question of the day, we would play Scrabble on my giant wall-mounted Scrabble board. But that left at least forty-five minutes of nothing on the Wednesday—a disaster in the making. How could I have let this happen? I lifted my eyes as I got up from the computer and they happened to hit *Greatness comes when we talk* scrawled across the whiteboard. *Yes, I can do this!*

Twenty minutes later my freshmen were sharing their journal writes in which they had responded to that quote:

> *If we did not communicate most of what we have now wouldn't exist.*
>
> —Jackie S

> *. . . the power of words. We were given a voice for a reason— greatness could be it, depending on what you have to say.*
>
> —Taylor X

> *. . . when a person is feeling down, all it takes is for someone to talk to them. The power of talking creates greatness.*
>
> —Andrew L

> *Sometimes evil or bad things may come when we talk, but good things come more.*
>
> —Jake M

> *I think the reason greatness comes when we talk is because*

you get to hear some of the great ideas people have and share some of those ideas.

—Devon B

The more you talk to someone the happier you're going to be.

--Heaven B

. . . thinking is where greatness is formed—talking is when it's shared.

—Kyle P

And then John volunteered to share his response. Now it isn't as though John never shares his work because he does. Neither is it that he's a low achiever and he shocked us with abnormal greatness. No, this was just one of those times when a kid commanded his audience:

When two minds talk, great things can happen. When people talk we find new ways of doing almost anything, from inventions in modern science to new English words. Maybe a new mapping device to get accurate maps, times, and distances.

We find new ways to go about helping troubled kids, fix broken transportation and machinery. We find new ways to plow the field and house the cattle.

We find new medicines, new ways to cure diseases and other health issues. We find new ways to make that hospital better, or the ambulance to get there, even down to making the waiting line move faster.

We can even find ways to make our education better and lower the dropout rate. We can find ways to make schools safer and ways to make the food better and healthier—and get that lunch line to move quicker as well.

--John R

There was rapt silence when John finished reading and looked up. Somebody, actually several together I think, said, "Wow!" which was quickly followed by applause. John smiled—and reddened. I went over to his seat and marked his response with the top score, a check-plus-plus (I later added another plus!).

See, that's one of the things about teaching. I might have had what I thought was the most well thought out, designed, and executed lesson plan—and it could have flopped, like our "no electronic devices in school" policy. Here I was trying to pull something out of my armpit to keep the class moving forward and it went over like we'd just taken cell phones off that list—who would have thought! You know, it occurs to me that maybe it's okay to run out of lesson plans once in a while . . . or maybe I should just let them talk more.

This column originally appeared in Foster's Daily Democrat, Dover, NH on January 17, 2008.

I Wish I'd Written That

There are so many things I love about teaching, and particularly about teaching English. It seems like the academic discipline of English allows me to get to know my students in ways that some other disciplines may not so readily permit—through their writing, and they do a lot of it for me. Now does that mean I actually look forward to spending hundreds of hours outside of class each semester grading papers some other teachers may not have? No, it definitely does not, but that's part of the job.

Now I'm pretty sure I've mentioned that one of the things which thrills me is when I read a student's paper and find myself saying, "Wow! I wish I'd written that." Like the time I asked students to react to the word "mistakes." Daryl wrote, "Make mistakes. Not too many, not too few. Living a life without them makes you fragile." I like that. I wish I'd written it. Or how about this line that I pulled from one of Chris's papers one year when we were writing about *compassion*: "The possession of compassion is irrelevant when one lacks the will to release it." I wish I'd written that. Or how about this one from Logan when we were reacting to the philosopher Schopenhauer's *Man is the universe greatly reduced*: "The universe seemingly goes on forever and our minds can in theory do the same." Then there was Becky's take on the relevance of history. "If you say that the history of people's lives is meaningless then you might as well think of your life as meaningless, because your life will become the history looked back on." I wish I'd written those, too.

More recently I gave an assignment to my senior honors students who were about to complete a unit called "On Death and

Dying." During the unit we read *Tuesday's with Morrie*, watched the movie Dad, with Ted Danson and Olympia Dukakis," and spent a lot of time discussing and writing about our own mortality and that of those we love. We talked and wrote about our fear of dying and how we *live* with that. We shared stories with each other about family members and friends who had died, and how those experiences helped define who we have become. Some years I actually had each of us write our own obituary, focusing on how we would want to be remembered.

One of my writing assignments this year used the following prompt: Write a one-page paper titled Remembering . . . (fill in the name) in which you share detailed memories of someone you know personally who has died. What follows is a response to that prompt by Bryan who, aside from being my student and a great hockey player, has for several years also worked as a dietary aide at an assisted living facility.

Remembering Clara*

A strong sturdy voice can be heard throughout the dining room: "Where's my food!" A wrinkly old woman sits with her partner in crime *Roberta. They both swear like sailors, trying to get anyone's attention because they're hungry. Clara is a larger woman and she sits in a black and silver wheel chair, her thin arms and pencil fingers slam down on the table. Those harsh words utter from her mouth every, oh, ten seconds! She looks around with her big, thick pink-framed glasses, her dark eyeballs bulging to the size of half-dollars. She is a strong woman, not afraid to speak her mind—this was last year.

A soft voice can be heard in the corner of the dining room: "Where am I?" Clara sits alone now; her partner has given in to the cold sleep. She is no longer the large powerful woman she once was, she is a ghost in living form. Pale and white, the pencil thickness that was once in her fingers has moved into her wrists. Clara doesn't eat anymore, she is sliding into the softly cupped hands of death. People say their good-byes. She is now a weak woman in body, afraid of losing her mind—this was a month ago.

"Clara passed away, you can take her tray off the cart," a black haired nurse says from over a pink striped half wall. I pulled off her tray and wrote "Deceased" on her food card. I served supper, life went on. I came back to clean up the dishes, a gray haired man in a jean jacket walked by with a stretcher and an empty body bag. He signed papers, went into Clara's room, and wheeled out the stretcher about three minutes later. As he walked by time paused briefly. The body bag looked the same. Clara had become so thin she could hardly be seen. She was a strong woman, her mind now free. She was promoted from an "is" to a "was" in the span of a few hours—this was Friday.

Do you see what I mean? Without writing I might have missed Chris's compassion, and Logan's universal wisdom. I might never have seen history qualified in such concrete terms. If I didn't teach writing how would I have ever learned how much Bryan connects with his residents? How would I have discovered his ability to provide clear, vivid descriptions and in so doing capture not just details in his vocabulary but color, texture, admiration, respect, frustration, and sadness. Yes, I love to see Bryan's aggressiveness on the ice. But I also love to see his humor in the classroom and his tenderness in print. See? I have it all. And the hundreds of hours of grading? Shoot, I still feel guilty sometimes about how good I have it. Do I wish I'd written "Remembering Clara"? Kind of. But I'd never have done it justice.

* Not her real name

This column originally appeared in Foster's Daily Democrat, Dover, NH on March 29, 2007.

Friends, Family, and 55

I am not going to pretend that there aren't "those days" no matter how much I love my kids and my job. When a reading assignment gets blown off or someone fails to turn in a paper on time, I'll admit it, I get ticked. When a student refuses to comply with a reasonable request—like reading aloud in class, for example, or answering a simple question—I get really ticked. On the rare occasions that students disrespect each other I get really, really ticked! But the truth is, most of the time those things don't happen. Most days we have a pretty good time and accomplish a lot in my classes, and the 90 minutes is gone—in about half that time.

Then there are the days when it is just plain fun to be in my room, like the day we do the "All-Aboard" game or the human knot. All-Aboard is an incentive exercise where everyone in the group has to have at least one foot on this 24 inch square platform and the other foot off the floor. They have to talk, strategize, think, regroup, hold on to each other. There is fear, trepidation, determination, and lots of laughter. Same thing with the human knot—they have to talk to each other, think about the next move. There is concentration, twisting, turning, rotating grips, sweat, and sticky hands, yet still lots of fun and laughter.

There was the day I gave Bobby back a test—with a ninety! The day Ricco told Ms. Pepin that she was his hero—at least for the day! And how about the Sunday afternoon I called Alyssa? I could hear the "Oh no, not again," in her voice.

"Hey, Alyssa, it's me."

"Hi, Mr. Mac. What's up!"

"Alyssa, how many times this semester have you had to rewrite a paper for me before I would grade it?"

"A lot of times!"

"Well guess what? You don't have to this time! I thought you might like to know that you did a nice job on this paper, and I'm wicked proud of you." What a fun day we had on Monday.

Then there was the time when the question of the day was something like, *if you could choose immortality at what age would you choose it?*

Now as you might imagine there were myriad answers. Some were satisfied to be eighteen for the rest of eternity. Others wanted to be twenty-one, for obvious reasons, and still others were willing to push it to twenty-five when insurance rates go down. A few, I think, even went as far as thirty.

Corey was the one who blew my mind. "Corey, if you could choose immortality at what age would you choose it?" I queried.

He looked at me in all seriousness and replied, "fifty-five."

"Are you serious?" I responded as most of the rest of the class indicated their disbelief. "I mean, Corey, I've had a lot of students say they wanted to be a lot of ages over the years, but I know I've never before had a student who wanted to be fifty-five!" And most of his friends started giving him all kids of grief about such a "ridiculous" answer.

"No, come on, think about it you guys. Almost everybody I know who is fifty-five has things all set. They have jobs they like and have a lot of experience at, they have families, they made it through all the crap of their growing up years, but are still young enough to enjoy life. They just seem really happy and content with their lives. Man, I'm telling ya, I can't wait to be fifty-five!"

See, that's part of the fun. Just when you think you've got them figured out, when you think you've got a response for every bizarre little quirk and twist they can display, one of them redefines bizarre. I loved it—fifty-five!

Of course, then it was my turn.

"Good morning, Mr. MacKenzie," somebody said, "how are

you this morning?"

"You know, if I was any better, I'd be perfect!"

"That's great. So, if you could choose immortality, at what age would you choose it?"

"I want to answer the question, but before I do, I'd like to know what you think I'm going to say."

Most of them thought I'd want to be younger, like many middle-aged people. You know, less gray hair, smoother skin, whiter teeth, fewer aches and pains.

The average guess was around twenty-five.

"Well," I finally responded, "I'd like to think I would have brains enough to never choose immortality, but if I didn't and I was going to choose, I choose right now." There were some surprised faces.

"Look you guys, I hated turning thirty, dreaded it from the day I turned twenty- nine. But I've smartened up since then. I didn't mind turning forty a bit and I was almost proud of turning fifty. I mean, what the heck, I'm still here, got all my parts, everything still works—I'm not doin' too bad.

Besides, I don't want to sacrifice one moment of my life, one relationship, one friend, or one relative. If I chose even forty-five, for example, I'd lose every single one of you. If I chose thirty-nine I'd lose every student I ever had and the hundreds of resulting friendships. If I chose twenty-one I'd lose my wife, my stepchildren and my grandchildren. No I'm not willing to sacrifice any of my life to be younger."

Now in case he happens to be reading this, "Corey, I still can't tell how I like fifty-five, "cause I'm not there yet. If I'm lucky I'll let you know in four-and-a-half years." When I do turn fifty-five though, I'll bet I'll still be having fun, especially if I'm still teaching, and I know it'll beat the heck out of the alternative.

This column originally appeared in Foster's Daily Democrat, Dover, NH on February 28, 2008.

Writing with Passion

I called one of my sophomores last Sunday afternoon. He likely assumed I was calling to deliver some kind of bad news. What I wanted was to tell John that I'd just read his paper and that it was probably the best paper he'd ever written for me during the two courses we'd had together. "Make no mistake," I said, "the paper has lots of problems in terms of construction, which we need to correct, but for content, it's an excellent personal narrative."

What John had done was follow some advice I always give my students about their writing, especially personal writing: *people always write best when they write about things for which they feel passion.* If you knew John as I have known John, as an underachiever, always tired, usually behind in his work, and bursting with apathy then you would understand why this paper came across as more than a personal narrative. What follows is a somewhat condensed version.

I Can't Stand This

One of the many problems I have is that I don't care enough about the things that matter in life—like grades. I can't tell you why I have stopped caring about my grades but one reason may be because for the past ten years of school it's been all about getting that A, not about how I got there . . . Another reason could be that now I am in classes with very smart people who can do an assignment in half the time it takes me and with half the effort. It makes me very frustrated when I can't do work at the same speed or as well as other people. Then when I go home to finish my homework I can never concentrate on it; I get distracted by wanting to go outside and have fun, watch the internet or surf the web for no other reason than to avoid my homework . . . .

Some people say that stress is a problem to all, and if people have too much stress it can hurt them mentally and physically, and may cause them to become frustrated easily. This could affect me because when I lie down to go to sleep my mind races about everything I should have done during the day or could have done better. I think about having to live up to my brother and do as well or better than him, wanting to fit in with my friends, trying to live up to my parents' expectations, wanting to do good in sports, and prove to my teachers that I am a good student. These may be the reasons I can't sleep well at night. I hate it when my mind races and thinks about things I haven't done or about what I did wrong.

In the past three weeks I have been getting an average of 4-6 hours of sleep—and going to bed early doesn't help because it just gives me more time to think about all those problems. Then in class I can't concentrate (because I'm so tired), like when a teacher is talking about what we will be doing, and explaining how to do it, I will start to zone off. This could be one of the reasons I am bad at math, because I didn't hear what to do or even what page we were on in the book. It's not a day dream; it's more of a thought process. I'll be thinking about how I pissed off a teacher, or how we will never use this in our lives. Why do I need to write poetry or worry about what happens to some kid in a story when I'm going to be an engineering major? Then the worst thing happens: a teacher suddenly brings you back into class with a question, and you have no idea how to respond . . . .

[Another problem I have is] having four teachers ninety minutes a day for ninety days . . . I just hate the same things day after day after day. Like as I'm writing this paper I have moved around at least ten times in a half hour, had three drinks, and the song on my iPod is never the right one [so I'm constantly changing tunes].

Another problem I have is I always wait until the last minute. I don't call it procrastination because I try to do it but I just can't concentrate on anything—ever. When I had the MAP tests I took a five minute break and just sat there looking around, because I didn't want to continue reading the long stories and answering the questions about them.

Now you might never have thought that John Smith (not his real name) can't concentrate in class. It took a lot of work for me to say these things—to anyone let alone my teacher. My brother doesn't know that I want to be like him because I don't know how to show it. My parents don't know I worry about meeting their expectations. So while this is a paper I had to write for my crazy Mr. Mac, it is also a peek into the life of a hyper, fun-crazed, routine hating teenager's life, and a story someone needed to tell from the kid's point of view. The kids are the ones who have the control, who must make the changes to make things better or worse for themselves. Most at this age don't know what to do to dig their way out of their over caffeinated, stressed-to-the-limit lives. These are the lives that, when you open your paper in ten years, will be in the obituaries—or making front-page news for world changing leaps in medicine.

See what I mean? See why I was so proud (and stunned)? If he'd written with any more passion *I* couldn't stand it!

This column originally appeared in Foster's Daily Democrat, Dover, NH on June 16, 2009.

I Want to Know What You Think

All three of my classes turned in their research papers today, the final day of school before April vacation. Some of the kids came in all smiles breathing the cliché "sigh of relief." Others came in still sweating, asking, "Mr. MacKenzie, my printer wouldn't work right; can I go down to the library to print off my paper?" Still others were dripping even more profusely, almost begging to "turn it in by 2:30," or "email it to [me] by the end of the day." I finally caved, as usual, and told all those who hadn't turned it in during class that if I had it on my desk by the time I left school or in my email by the time I went to bed, I'd still accept it for full credit. After that all bets were off.

Before leaving school this afternoon, I took a look through the piles. I had papers supporting the Iraq war and opposing it. I had papers advocating for gay marriage, and some writing against it. I had papers on endangered species, school uniforms, global warming, and rules governing electronic devices in school. They are now on vacation. I get to go to work—reading and assessing.

Now I probably ought to tell you that most of my students, whether they are in regular English I or Honors English IV, look forward to writing a research paper about as much as they look forward to paying car insurance. For my freshmen it was a standard five-paragraph essay with a minimum of two sources from which they must find quotes that support their thesis. For the sophomores it was a three to five page paper with three to five sources. And the papers must be written using proper MLA formatting and documentation style.

The most difficult concept for many of them with this paper

is avoiding the trap of writing a "report." "No," I say, "this is not a 'report;' reports are things you write on books in the fifth grade. This is a thesis driven research paper. Your job is to add something new to the discussion. That means I *don't* want you to go out there and find out everything you can on your topic and then puke it back to me 'in your own words.' Why would I need you to do that? If I only wanted to know what your sources thought I'd go directly to them. No offense, they're probably better writers than you, better than me for that matter. I want to know what *you* think about some aspect of your topic. The sources are only there to support *your* ideas, not the other way around."

Of course the next question always is, "Can you give us an example?" And then the teaching of thesis statements begins. This year I said that if I were going to write a research paper on global warming my thesis statement might be something like *When examining the global temperature patterns over the last century, the predicted catastrophic damage to the planet from rising temperatures may be the biggest hoax ever perpetrated on the general public.* The topic is global warming. The thesis statement, which drives my research paper, is my belief.

Let's say my topic is school uniforms (a favorite of mine since I'm tired of telling boys to pull their pants up and girls to button their tops up). I might craft a thesis statement that read something like this: *Given the plethora of information available regarding the greatly improved rates of reduction in school violence, sexual harassment, dropouts, failures, and the like, school boards, whose sole duty is to provide the best education possible for their children, that have not adopted a school uniform policy are being irresponsible in their duties.*

One year I used parental licensing as a topic idea. The kids wanted to know what the heck I was talking about. I said, think about it you guys. The people who install the wiring in your house to provide electricity have to be licensed, because the wiring has to be safe. The people who put the pipes together to bring the water into your house and take the doo doo away have to be licensed, because, after all, we don't want to have leaks and back-ups that might be health hazards. Yet any two people, brilliant or boneheads, can get together and make a baby—that the rest of us may then have to deal with in any number of ways. Was I being serious? Not completely, but it did spark an interesting discussion about the possibility of mandatory parenting classes in high school.

Well, tomorrow morning I'll begin reading. From what they said when turning their papers in, I know that most of those who wrote on the war are suggesting, for a variety of reasons, that we need to get out of Iraq. I know that one of my most fashion conscious students chose to write about school uniforms—because she is adamantly opposed to them. She's even opposed to a strict dress code. I am also not expecting to see many thesis statements that suggest "global warming," excuse me, "climate change" is a bunch of hooey. And you know, I was wrong; after a quick glance there were not *some* papers opposing gay marriage, there was one. There is even one paper in which the student believes we need to responsibly finish what we've started in Iraq. The thing is, it's all good, since I don't care *what* my students think nearly as much as I care *that* they think.

Now, it's getting late and I have to go check my email—and probably refigure some bets.

This column originally appeared in Foster's Daily Democrat, Dover, NH on April 21. 2009.

Persuasion: Thinking About It

It's a Saturday afternoon and I spent my morning at my classroom desk reading and grading papers, five to seven page persuasive papers to be exact. I signed in on the after-hours log at 6:55 AM vowing to get ten papers done by noon. Well, I was close. I got on a roll and signed out at 11:50 with eleven done. Eleven papers from eleven different students on eleven different topics, all trying to convince me to agree with something.

In the first one, titled "The all too Common Split," the writer was talking about her parent's divorce and how she "watched [her dad] load up his van with all his things . . ." and how she "slept that night wondering what he was doing, and if he missed [her]." "Kids," she wrote "feel the repercussions of their parents' decisions every day, even if they don't show it." I read at least one of these papers every year.

I usually have some firsts, too. For example, Ron, a member of our football team, is trying to convince me that we make way too much out of steroid use among professional athletes. "[He's] not saying that steroids should be legalized . . ." just "that athletes shouldn't be punished so harshly for using them." On the surface that might sound like an odd position for a dedicated student athlete to take, but his rationale is interesting. He argues, "Steroids just make you stronger; they don't give you more talent at what you do." In other words, "Baseball players want to hit the ball farther, but if you can't hit [in the first place] then what does it matter?" Was I convinced after reading his paper? No—but I'm thinking about it.

Of course I am convinced that people spend way too much

time online in any number of mind-numbing, impersonal ways. So Laura was able to hook me with just her title: *The Internet: Friend Request Denied*. She started off her paper suggesting that "the communication of teens today differs greatly from those of the preceding generation. The reason: The Internet. With AIM, Facebook, and Twitter, just to name a few, adolescents become quickly informed on the latest great gossip in a matter of minutes, even seconds. Rumors spread faster and private conversations can be copied, pasted, and posted on any public site . . . Many young people have become less social in the real world because of social networking [in the cyber world]." Many have tried, unnecessarily, to convince me of the dangers of the World Wide Web, but rarely are they under thirty, and never have they been teenagers. I've thought about both Facebook and Twitter. Now I think I'll *stop* thinking about them.

Gina's paper wants us to think in another direction. Last year our administration wanted to do away with senior class trips. This year they've *done* away with senior class trips. Gina, a senior, is understandably not happy about that. She wrote that "like all other students in high school [she has] always wondered what [they] will do for [their] senior trip and how [they] will celebrate [their] last few days as the Somersworth High School class of 2010. It was just recently that [she] discovered [they] will not have the choice of planning [their] end-of-the-year trip." She went on to say she thinks "this is a huge privilege that has been taken away . . . and [they] should have the same opportunities every other class has had." I'm convinced, but my power ends with grading the paper.

Neither do I have the power to comply with another writer who penned her displeasure with homework. I get these papers every year, but I must say the persuading ammunition this time around was more creative. I hope Jane's mother understands how much her daughter hates it that she is unable help out with all the household chores her mother struggles with because of all her "useless" homework. Maybe I should tell her myself, so she doesn't think this girl is just being lazy and uncaring.

There was another paper that really got me to thinking. It was Neb's paper. Neb is a senior who is studying to be an electrician, and his idea is for the Tri-city area to start a "Trade School." He believes that if Dover, Somersworth, and Rochester pooled their resources they could relocate and merge their three Career Technical Centers into one regional trade school that would serve a certain segment of the student population for whom the traditional high school, with its traditional academic focus, is just not working. You know what? The idea isn't all that crazy. Nobody has enough money, maybe pooling our resources is a good idea. It is not necessary, nor even desirable, for all students go through the same educational mold. Yes, I wish they all liked and would learn Shakespeare, and how to write a five to seven page essay, but they don't and they won't. Why not have a school that focuses on career training with revised academics? It works at the college level so why not at the secondary level? I'm not sure if you've persuaded me yet Neb, but you've convinced me to think about it.

That's really enough for most students, you know. They're okay if they don't completely change our minds, they just don't want to be completely dismissed without thought. Kids want us to know our actions sometimes hurt them. They want us to know they don't always agree with us. They want us to know that they are capable of coming up with some really interesting ideas . . . about family and the Internet and class trips and drugs and education. They don't *have* to change our minds, they just want us to think about it.

This column originally appeared in Foster's Daily Democrat, Dover, NH on October 20,. 2009.

What Are You Waiting For?

I'm writing this piece in early December, 2008, when it seems everybody is waiting for something. Jews are waiting for Chanukah. Christians are waiting to celebrate the birth of Jesus. This year Muslims have been waiting for the Hajj and Eid-al-Adha (though most of the waiting was in November), while Buddhists were waiting (again, mostly in November) for Bodhi Day. Some Africans are waiting for Kwanza, which will be celebrated for the forty-third time in 2008, and according to a Vanderbilt Website "is secular, not religious, and aims to strengthen African cultural identity and community values while providing a spiritual alternative to the commercialism of Christmas."

Throughout the country most little kids are waiting for Santa Claus, and most older kids are waiting for school vacation. College students are waiting for finals and many high school seniors are waiting to become college students. Skiers are waiting for snow and football fans are waiting for the playoffs. Shoppers are waiting in check-out lines and retailers are waiting to see their year-end profit and loss statements. Taxpayers are already waiting for their 2008 refunds, teachers are waiting to collapse for a few days, and almost everybody is waiting for presents, especially General Motors, Ford, and Chrysler. Me? I'm just waiting to be warm again.

Yes, we do a lot of waiting this time of year, and I don't know about you but I don't wait well. I don't like to wait in lines at restaurants. I don't like to wait for phone calls or people who are late or out-of-stock merchandise or haircuts or oil changes. I like things to happen *now*. See I tend to get very irritated when I have to wait for things. I don't like it when meetings start late, or concerts, or movies, or church. I don't like to wait for kids to quiet down so we can start class or for papers or homework that don't come in on time. And I *really* can't stand it when people don't show up for an appointment.

What I need to do, though, is concentrate less on the waiting and more on the anticipation. Take the other day. After I finally got my freshmen to sit down, shut their mouths (sort of), and focus we had a really good class. Instead of worrying about the wait for my tax refund (which I probably won't get anyway) I could spend the time getting excited about how to use it. I remember a course I had one time at UNH. The assignment was to write a short response to a prompt dealing with *anticipation*. One of my classmates wrote this terrific piece about that brief but intense period of anticipation leading to your first kiss. His point was that the anticipation was, in a way, more exciting than the actual event. When I think about it, the getting ready period for our annual trip to the Dominican Republic is filled with great anticipation. We start packing early, weighing suitcases, and trying to decide what we *want* to bring versus what we can't live without. It doesn't beat getting off that plane in Puerto Plata and feeling instant summer, but it is exciting.

What I should also do is think more about stones and glass houses and the times when *I'm* the cause of the wait, like this last fall when my principal was waiting for me to show up for Freshmen Orientation, or when a couple was waiting over forty minutes at church for me to show up to go over wedding music with them. Let me just confess that it's a good thing my principal had a fall-back plan, and that the pastor of the church saw the couple waiting and called me. I'm also really glad that neither Ron, my barber, nor Pete, my mechanic, get nearly as worked up about my waiting as I do.

Sometimes that Native American moccasin proverb—it's not a bad idea. Waiting for a tax refund beats the heck out of waiting for an unemployment check. Waiting for a $20 oil change means I have a functioning vehicle and I'm *not* waiting for a $2000 transmission. And you know the poems my freshmen wrote the other day, some of them were good enough they *almost* made the wait worth it. Then again, their lives aren't always perfect and punctual either. Some of them may be antsy because they're waiting for Christmas while others may be antsy because they know there won't *be* much Christmas. Even waiting for a haircut at Ron's or in a register line at Walmart, hey, at least I still have hair that needs to be cut and the money to buy a few Christmas presents.

The other day I was talking with a student who had been waiting for several weeks to hear if he received early acceptance at the college to which he'd applied—he didn't. What I found admirable, even comforting, though, was that he *knows* everything will be okay in the end, no matter how it works out. I was talking with another student who had been eagerly waiting, following last week's auditions, for the cast to be posted on the drama department's "call board," for this spring's musical—someone else's name was beside the part she'd hoped for. But while we talked she acknowledged that what was more important was being part of the production, a member of the cast, and a supporter of her other friends in the show. That's what Christmas, and life, is really all about, making a difference for someone else. I think I'll go give my wife a kiss, send a thank you card to my principal, give thanks I don't own any GM stock, then go buy a couple of presents for "someone else." After that, I think I'll just hunker down and wait for spring!

This column originally appeared in Foster's Daily Democrat, Dover, NH on December 23, 2008.

PART VI

BEYOND THE CLASSROOM

Nobody has ever been foolish enough to actually say it to my face, but I know there are those out there in "taxpayer" land who claim that *teachers are really paid very well when you consider that they only have a part-time job anyway.* Are you kidding me? One would have to either be on a total power trip or an absolute moron to believe that. I would challenge anyone to follow me for a month and see how just how *part-time* my job is! Most people probably couldn't keep up with me—even though they're just watching. Part-time! I actually ran the numbers somewhere in my first semester of teaching when I had moved from "the dreaded private sector" to public education. Let me just say that I worked way more hours teaching, even with summers and school vacation weeks off, than I had as a food service district manager—and made way less money.

Now, if my teaching job only involved my time in the classroom, sure, I would have a part-time job: about seven hours a day, five days a week, for about thirty-eight weeks a year. In reality, those hours typically account for a little more than half of what is required for me to properly and responsibly do my job.

I spend countless hours a year in meetings, most are mandatory (department, faculty, parent, assigned teams, etc.), and a few I am volunteered for. Many additional hours, outside of the school day, are necessary for grading student work in the required "timely manner." For example, when I would get in a two-class set of five to seven page personal narratives, I was good for a minimum of twenty-five hours of grading, most often more—if I did a decent job and gave good feedback. And let's not forget the things I get *asked* to do, like chaperone student events, attend games or concerts or shows, contribute to a school board or city council meeting. I'm not whining, mind you, but those things are all part of the job. It's not unlike when you get married. You're not just marrying a person, you're marrying into another family—and with that comes additional family responsibilities.

Let me say, too, that those "after hours" responsibilities don't come stress-free! One time I was chaperoning a weekend trip to Washington, DC. Students (seniors, by the way) were given the afternoon to visit any of the museums in the Smithsonian complex. All of a sudden one of the other chaperones gets a ding on her cell, and low and behold we see a Facebook post from one of our kids, including a picture of a small group who had hailed a cab and gone to Hooters. Yeah, that went over really big with my superintendent.

I have spent time going to a kid's farm to watch him birth a calf, going to the Strafford County jail to help a kid finish two courses while incarcerated, local hospitals to provide encouragement, even the Jehovah's Witness' Kingdom Hall for a special celebration, about which I knew absolutely nothing, but my student had invited me. Recently I made several trips to a student's house to help him finish The Odyssey, Romeo and Juliet, and his research paper. During some of the visits I had to wear a surgical mask because the student's chemotherapy had weakened his immune system, but he was determined not to fall behind in school. The hours I spend doing those things require sacrificing my own personal time—or more accurately my family's time. Some of them I have to do to be a teacher. The others I only have to do if I want to be a good teacher.

Welcome to Hades

Since the literature focus in English IV at Somersworth High School is world lit, and since a rather lengthy excerpt from Dante's "Inferno" is included in our senior anthology, it was a convenient text with which to work. For those of you unfamiliar with Dante Alighieri's trilogy, *The Divine Comedy*, "Inferno" is the leg of the trip through Hades, or the Underworld. Dante's vision of the Underworld is layered; the worse one's sins in life, the lower the descent, hence the cliché of telling someone "to which layer of Dante's Hell they might go."

I figured there had to be a more creative way of experiencing Dante's work than simply reading the individual cantos or chapters in class, particularly given the beautifully creative and figurative, but stilted and somewhat archaic, diction and syntax. So I approached my then pastor, Rev. Anne Robertson, to toss around some ideas. I figured who could know more about Satan's hide-a-way than a pastor, right? After all, they spend much of their lives trying to keep the rest of us out of it. Being familiar with Dante's work, and having had a secret desire to both travel more and act, Anne decided to lead a dramatic "trip" with me, she as Virgil, Dante's tour-guide, and me as the bard. On the day of departure we donned our traveling clothes, black velvet robes and high necked, ruffle collared white shirts, and began our descent to Purgatory and beyond.

As my students arrived at "the gate," they were greeted by the infamous admonition "Abandon All Hope, Ye Who Enter Here." They took their seats in a cool, almost black room backlit with red light, eerily diffused by the low lying smoke rolling through the room. Shortly they were listening to the lines of

Dante's opening confession:

"Midway in our life's journey, I went astray / from the straight road and woke to find myself / alone in a dark wood. How shall I say / what wood that was! I never saw so drear, / so rank, so arduous a wilderness! / Its very memory gives shape to fear."

Fortunately for Dante, his confession and fear brought forth the person of Virgil, who served as his guide on a journey through the Underworld and out the other side, as a means of showing him his way back to the "True Way." But what a journey it was.

As the smoke rolled across the floor and dissipated, Dante's ears were met with "sighs and cries and wails coiled and recoiled / on the starless air, spilling [his] soul to tears. / A confusion of tongues and monstrous accents toiled / in pain and anger." And he beseeched of Virgil, "what souls are these who run through this black haze?"

Despite their obvious anguish, consider Dante's surprise when he discovered that he was only seeing Limbo, reserved for those who could not achieve salvation because of lack of baptism. Next came the second circle, reserved for "those who sinned in the flesh, the carnal and lusty / who betrayed reason to their appetite. And the third contained the gluttonous, who did nothing more with the gifts of God than eat and drink, producing only piles of garbage—thus they were surrounded with it. Then there was level four, for the hoarders and wasters weighed down with heavy boulders against which they would spend all eternity pushing and straining.

The trip grew foggier and the red mist became hotter still as we moved to the fifth layer and the muck and slime of the River Styx, which mires the souls of the wrathful as they violently attack each other. Then on to the sixth layer and the capitol city of Hades, Dis, home of the heretics who denied God's existence and eternal life, and are therefore put to eternal death. We move through the home of the violent and the fraudulent, finally arriving at the ninth layer, where upon our arrival we see "The sinner [raise] his mouth from his grim repast / and [wipe] it on the hair of the bloody head / whose nape he had all but eaten away.

"Why," someone asked later, "would a count gnaw at the head and brains of an archbishop?"

"Well," I respond, "that's how Dante thought God might deal with two evil people, one whose appetite for power resulted in the second's death by starvation. The one serves as the everlasting food for the other, the everlasting hungry.

Ultimately, as Dante's eyes have been wrenched open, our smoke, dim redness, and dark give way to the light of the world again, and "My Guide and I [cross] over and [begin] / to mount that little known and lightless road / to ascend into the shining world again." Anne and I, too, made it through, though our shining light did come from a switch on the wall.

Why go through all of this to study a piece of fourteenth-century Italian poetry, one might ask? Well, the tough diction and syntax aside, remember what they say about the worth of a picture. This way my students could experience the literature rather than just read it. But, one might also ask, really, what can ancient literature offer us today? Are you kidding me? It still reeks of all that *is* good literature: challenge, intrigue, death, life, destruction, retribution, religion, the disgusting, the sensual, the divine, and in this case one man's vison of God's punishment for the unfaithful. What more could you ask for in a piece of literature? Is it my students' conception? Doubtful, but hopefully useful. In the end Dante finds the path back to The True Way and "walked out once more beneath the stars." Me? Well, I've never been much of a glutton and I'm pretty sure I've never caused anyone's death, but you can bet I'll be in church Sunday. I'm taking as few chances as possible.

This column originally appeared in Foster's Daily Democrat, Dover, NH on June 17, 2008.

All the Other Stuff

There was a letter posted in the teacher's room recently reminding anyone considering retiring at the end of this school year to submit a letter of intent by December 1st. Over my lifetime I have known a lot of teachers who have retired, many of them early. I've always found it interesting that few retired because of the kids. No, they have, by their own admission, retired because of meetings and committees and study groups and new initiatives and programs and workshops and staff development, and IEP meetings and parent conferences and . . . Well, you get the idea; they didn't retire because they were tired of the kids, but because they were tired of all the other stuff they were required or "invited" to do.

This week I had Curriculum Council after school on Monday, my own department meeting after school on Tuesday, my PBIS Targeted Team meeting after school on Wednesday. Next week it is the Leadership Team on Tuesday followed by an association meeting. The next week it's a faculty meeting on Tuesday, Targeted Team again on Wednesday, an IEP meeting on Thursday, and it goes on and on.

This coming Friday I have to miss all of my classes to attend a PLATO training workshop. Now you might think, *what the heck, so he's got to attend a workshop—he doesn't have to attend classes that day!* While that is true, it will take me at least an hour to write up sub plans. And even after I've done a detailed set of sub plans and laid out all the required materials, I still spend half the time I'm away from my classes worrying about being away from my classes.

Now don't misunderstand me—I'm not whining; I'm simply

stating the reality of a teacher's life. And I have it easier than many, since I only have a half-time contract, which means I only work a half year. But that's not even really true, because while I'm gone for a little over half of second semester I'm still the department head so I am working electronically off and on during the entire three-month absence, and then I get home just in time to dive into the scheduling and course assignment process for the next year. So while I only have a teaching load for half the year I'm still working.

Several years ago my high school went through the accreditation process. We spent over two years preparing for it. One of the few things we were called down on was our dropout rate. As a result I devoted my next three-year staff development cycle to finding ways to reduce our dropout rate. I spent several hundred hours working toward that goal.

My first year at Somersworth the NH Department of Education (DOE) had just adopted the New Hampshire frameworks as the new curriculum guidelines and we spent many, many hours aligning our curriculum to those Frameworks. Within a very few years the DOE had drafted the Grade-Span Expectations (GSEs) and English departments across the state shifted their alignments to the GSEs. My district, at the recommendation of our Assistant Superintendent in charge of curriculum, asked us to reformat the GSEs into a more user friendly document. We did that. Less than two years later the DOE has mandated that all NH high schools have competencies in place for every course they offer by the beginning of the 2008/2009 academic year. These competencies are being aligned to the GSEs, our school-wide expectations (mandated by the New England Association accreditation committee), and Competency Based Performance Standards. My department is a little over half done. I have a reasonable hope that we will make the deadline, though many districts likely will not. When we're done we will have several hundred hours invested in the process!

Are you beginning to see why many educators opt for early retirement? I can and I'm only fifty, with eleven years in teaching! The six-and-a-half hours a day in the classroom? Shoot, that's the easy part. My department is already wondering what the next initiative will be, when it will arrive, and how many hours, weeks, or months we will have to devote to it! Early retirement? I'll admit I've thought about it.

But another initiative is not what arrived next, it was an email from Melissa, a member of the class of 2000, asking me if I would be willing to play the organ at her marriage to JJ, a member of the class of 2001. How cool is that? And that got me to thinking about some of the other "invitations" I've had. Christine (class of 2001) invited me one afternoon to visit the grave of a deceased classmate, Casey Walters, where we shared quiet time and a few tears. Tom (class of 1999) almost always asks me to breakfast or lunch when he's home. Curtis (class of 2007) invites me to breakfast every time he's home. Kevin (class of 2001) invited me to a concert at UNH. Alexis (class of 2002) invited me to her dance recital. Seth (class of 1998) invited me to his house for dinner—he cooked! Steven (class of 2009) invites me to play Cribbage during lunch regularly! I have been invited to high school and college graduation parties, restaurants, frat houses, Christmas and New Year's Eve parties, and "the barn." I've attended everything from funerals to Eagle Scout Courts of Honor to the birth of a calf to a special service at the Jehovah's Witness Kingdom Hall. Students and former students have invited me to go skiing, swimming, fishing, Christmas Caroling, and sky diving. Early retirement . . . all the "other stuff" . . . hum . . . You know, if I have to have all the other stuff to get this stuff—I think I'll keep teaching a while longer.

This column originally appeared in Foster's Daily Democrat, Dover, NH on December 8, 2007.

Weekends Off

Typically a school kid's least favorite day of the week is Monday. We have hump day on Wednesdays, when many are saying, "Hey, at least we're half way to another school-free weekend!" And of course we have TGIF on Fridays, where every kid in school is saying, "Thank God! Get me 'outta' here!" So just to be different, last year I established Mystery Mondays for my freshmen. Every Monday I would do something special for them. One week I baked brownies, another time I did an adaptation of the verse "Make new friends but keep the old, one is silver and the other's gold," and gave it to each of them on a note card with a pre-1965 silver dime attached (I must confess it did aggravate me a bit when one of them saw the dime and said, "Hey, will this work in the vending machines in the caf?"). We did apple crisp one Monday and another I gave each student a marble along with this poem my wife MaryAnne had picked up at some meeting:

The Marble Story

A friend of mine once said to me this marble is for you!
For I was sure I'd lost all mine, when life became so blue.

So now I know, despite the odds, my marbles may be few,
That friend of mine reminded me life can be awesome too!

So I give you this marble just to have a little fun;
When others claim you've "lost your marbles"
At least you'll have this one!

Okay, so after we've gone through the school week, what about those weekends? Well, the one just past was pretty busy for me. I knew I had to finish grading my seniors' essays, since I had told them when they came in on the 14th that I'd have them back by the 24th. By Friday I was down to about fifteen from forty-five. I managed about three hours worth (five papers-ish) Friday evening, and then Saturday sandwiched in about another four hours worth around our weekend guests, a niece and her husband and their two children ages four and almost two. That left me about three more hours' worth for Sunday, so I had to do a little dealing with God.

I got to church early, about 7:00 am, to finish practicing my organ pieces for the 10:30 service and get my praise chorus music ready on the synth for the 9:00. Now at 10:30 I'm in the sanctuary for the entire time, but I have more flexibility for the early service. Once the praise music is done I don't *have* to do anything else until time to accompany the choir anthem, which comes late in the order of worship. Usually I go sit with my wife during the service, until the anthem. Today, however, I sat out in the back hall and got one-and-a-half more papers done. That left three-and-a-half.

Fortunately, my stepson, who was coming to visit his cousins, was late getting to the house and he was bringing the main dish for dinner. So sitting on the back porch midst two kids, a half deflated red rubber ball and a slightly used yellow Tonka dump truck I managed to get the half and one more full paper finished before dinner arrived—Alright, down to two!

But all was not good, for earlier that Sunday morning I discovered I had somehow forgotten we had our first Christmas Cantata rehearsal from 4:00 to 6:00 that afternoon. I also remembered that the next day was Monday—our third Monday since school began and I hadn't remembered a mystery yet. So I took the little kids and my eight-year-old grandson for ice cream after dinner (something for which I have become famous with the nieces, nephews, and grandchildren in the family), scrapped a side trip I had planned so my nephew could see the two new spec houses we are building, got the kids back home, and headed out for my rehearsal—still two papers short of completion.

Thank goodness the rehearsal ended early so I got home about 5:45—in time to have supper with everybody before the relatives headed back to New York and I headed out to school for our 7:00 Sunday night volleyball games. After about an hour-and-a-half of serves, passes, sets, and kills (like we ever really make that happen!) I skip back home to serve up the trash and recycling and kill off the last of my grading. By 9:00 I'm ready to tackle the papers, determined to have them finished for Monday morning. Thirty minutes later I'm about half way through the first paper and it occurs to me that if I'd stayed on the organ bench during the second service, where I'm virtually hidden from the congregation, I could have ticked off another half a paper and I'd be almost done now, which would have been really convenient as I have just remembered, yet again, that tomorrow is Monday—Mystery Mondays, remember? Of course it has also occurred to me that I'd probably have been pushing my deal with God a bit too far if I'd blown off both services for school work. So, what to do? It's too late to go buy marbles, I don't think I have twenty-five silver dimes left, and we ate all the apples over the weekend. "Hun!" I holler to my wife, "Do we have any cake mixes?" Well, thank goodness for my wife—she baked and frosted the cake and I stayed grading until I got to where I had one-half a paper left. I fell into bed sometime after 10:00 knowing I had more than enough time to finish it up before school—I mean I get there at 6:00 and classes don't start until 7:35. Weekends free? Shoot, I'm looking forward to Monday—so I can get some rest. Maybe I'm the one losing my marbles!

This column originally appeared in Foster's Daily Democrat, Dover, NH on September 27, 2007.

English and Alex

Alex had a slight limp coming off the soccer field as I was arriving to watch the second half of a home game just a few days after school had started. "Hey, Mr. Mac, do you want to massage my toes?" he asked as he walked toward me. Alex had just begun my Advanced Placement Language and Comp course and that was one of my earliest encounters with him. How does one respond to such a question? I would learn, for such questions were classic Alex, and I got them all the time—for the entire semester and beyond!

Even in class Alex would come out with the most random questions or comments, like the time I was peeling my apple early in the fall. We were working on some multiple choice questions as I peeled.

"So what do you guys think? Does the phrase 'His heart began to pant' best exemplify A) irony, B) personification, C) understatement, D) onomatopoeia, or E) metaphor?" I queried, reading from my AP teacher's manual.

"Are you going to eat those?" asked Alex.

I stopped talking and just sort of looked at him quizzically for a second or two. "Ah, I hadn't planned to," I said, quickly returning to my book.

"Is it okay if I do?" he pursued.

My look morphed to mild disbelief and I replied, "Sure, Alex, knock yourself out." And he began to eat my peels, as I moved back to the question at hand.

"I think it's personification," someone volunteered.

"I agree . . ."

"So, how come you peel your apples anyway," piped in Alex.

Another look of utter wonderment preceded my response of, "Not that it has anything even remotely to do with English but if you really must know it's because the peelings just get caught in my lousy teeth, which give me enough trouble as it is, and I can't get up and go floss them in the middle of class, and so to avoid all that I just peel the gosh darn apples—okay?"

"Sure, okay, I was just asking."

"Whatever. The answer key says that in the phrase 'His heart began to pant' the 'heart is given the human characteristic of breathing,' so the answer is *personification*, just as we thought."

The next day, as I handed out prompts for timed essay writing and then began nibbling on my apple, he asked again, "Is it okay if I have the peels?"

"Hey, Alex, go for it, buddy, whatever you want."

It quickly got to where he didn't even bother to ask. I peeled and he ate.

Then there was the time he came to my house for dinner. I had offered the class a choice between a day of swimming, games, and a cookout at my summer cottage or a full-course formal dinner at my real house in Somersworth—if anybody scored a 5 on the AP exam. See I'd had lots of 3s, and several 4s but I'd never had a student score a 5 before. They chose the formal dinner. Guess what? I had two 5s! If I'd known it would be that easy I'd have bribed the classes before them!

Anyway, we scheduled the dinner for the next Christmas break when they were all back from college. You should have seen them. The girls were all in evening wear and the guys in jackets and ties—well almost all the guys. Alex came in his traditional shorts and tee shirt. After serving virgin cocktails and hors d'oeuvres in the family room we moved to the dining room for dinner. The first words out of Alex's mouth as we gathered at the table were, "Hey, Mr. Mac, what fork and spoon do I use?" I looked at him, laughed, and replied, "The man scores a 3 on the AP English exam, a 5 on the AP calculus exam, and he asks what fork to use at the dinner table!"

So are you getting it? It's not as easy as some folks might think. We're almost always teaching, and even when we're not literally teaching we're really still teaching—just differently. See it's not all examples of parallel construction, scholarly diction and syntax, and identifying formal versus conversational voice. Every lesson doesn't deal with personal narratives, persuasion, or research. Sometimes we're setting examples of healthy food choices (even if we do peel away some of the best nutrients). We're being watched for self-control when the third announcement in ten minutes comes over the loud speaker interrupting my class, or three students don't have drafts ready for peer conferencing. And while at the AP level I don't usually have to explain the use of *your* and *you're*, or the difference between inductive and deductive reasoning, I may have to explain which fork to use for the salad or which spoon is for desert.

It's all good, though. Like that saying—how does it go? *From each according to his means to each according to his needs*, or something like that. Alex didn't need drilling on vocabulary. He had no trouble establishing his own voice in his writing, and he was pretty comfortable with issues of tone and audience. He did, however, need some help with his wardrobe and some training in table etiquette, the classroom table and the dining room table.

Oh yeah, and I almost forgot to tell you how I answered him. Remember, the toe massage question? I said, "Sure, Alex." He looked at me with amused disbelieve.

"Really?"

"Sure Alex." So he took his sneakers off and laid down on the grass. I figured, it was kind of like extended Biblical allusion— from literature to life; what the heck, if Jesus could wash the feet of twelve of his friends in an Upper Room, I could massage the toes of one of my students beside a soccer field.

This column originally appeared in Foster's Daily Democrat, Dover, NH on March 15, 2007.

A Glimpse of Next Year

The focus of this column from its conception has been to provide parents, students, teachers and the general taxpaying public a glimpse of what goes on inside one public high school English class. I want folks to read about the grammar lessons, the literature, the writing instruction, the critical thinking all swirling around and mixing into the academic discipline of English. And to provide that glimpse I have drawn on any number of assignments, books, lessons, discussions, celebrations, grievances, and student experiences which have become a part of my classroom at Somersworth High.

Many of those experiences are grounded in our personal stories, the events of our lives which form the basis of much of what we write. They bring their stories and I bring my mine—about family, friends, travels, or other life events. I tell about the time I almost killed my younger brother with a single-barrel shotgun (accidentally), about a job I had coveted, been assured of, and didn't get, about getting caught smoking when I was a kid, about the pasty tuna noodle casserole and canned diced carrots they used to serve us at Rollinsford Grade School. I could go on for pages. You see my students hear the stories of my past, which is what my readers have always gotten—stories of the past. Today, however, I shall deviate, for this story won't make it into my classroom until next year.

My deviation begins with a confession. The last several columns you have read were not sent to Foster's from Somersworth, for I have not been in Somersworth since January 29th. I have not even been in the United States since January 29th. No, my columns have been emailed in from our winter home in

Puerto Plata, Dominican Republic, to where my wife MaryAnne and I have moved at the end of each first semester since I went half-time—where I rarely need a jacket and *never* have to shovel snow! But let me get to the deviation.

No, it never snows in the Dominican Republic, but it does rain—boy does it rain. And the other night we had a good old-fashioned New England-style thunderstorm. You might have thought God had turned a multi-trillion gallon pail of water over and just dumped it, tossing in some great winds to boot. Within minutes I found that the floors everywhere there was a window open were flooded. It poured in under the door to the upstairs patio because the outside floor drains couldn't keep up with the volume. I discovered that when I heard the water running down the staircase into the living room. The cushions on the porch furniture got soaked before we could move them. I fussed and complained as I moved around the house throwing down towels to stop the water flow: the bottom of the stairs to protect a newly covered living room set and my digital piano, in front of the upstairs door to save the finish on the wood stairs, on the master bathroom floor to keep from breaking our necks, and in several other places threatened by the invading *lluvia*. Finally after shutting every door and window in the house and spreading every towel I could find on various floors I pulled back the spread and top sheet of my king-sized bed, flopped down, and complained myself to sleep: Jeezum crow! I come here to get tanned not waterlogged.

The next day I heard about areas nearby where there had been flash flooding. Our friend Ben called to say that both ends of the San Marcos bridge had been washed away. The terrific water flow was wreaking havoc with the public water supply, meaning we would be buying water for our cistern by the truckload for a while. Several streets in downtown Puerto Plata were under water and impassable. In general our winter respite was being disrupted and I didn't like it.

Then I remembered Miguel and his wife Pony, Dominican friends of ours who lived in a barrio called Javillar near the San Marcos River. To avoid getting the car stuck in its narrow, muddy streets, I drove to Javillar on my motorcycle to check on Pony and Miquel. Their modest cement house fairly near the river had suffered substantial damage but had withstood the flooding. They lost mattresses, bedding, and clothes but most of the bigger furniture survived. Then I thought about Javier, a friend in his late teens, and his father. I had only once been to their house, little more than a wood shack near the riverbank.

I made my way toward Javier's home, carefully stepping on randomly placed cinder blocks to stay above the mud of the narrow path. I was not prepared. As I rounded the corner my eyes were struck by piles of rubble, trash, and downed trees. Several dozen yards from where I stood children were already back into the muddy water splashing away. As I gazed, almost hypnotized, I was confronted by my previous evening's behavior, by my newly upholstered furniture and my digital piano and my water-laden tiled floors. Javier's house and everything in it, including the land on which it sat had been washed into the raging waters, its pieces strewn between Javillar and the open sea. I thought of our struggles to find enough towels the night before, and how useless all the towels in the world would have been in protecting Javier's home and furniture. I wondered what they would wear, how they would eat, where they would bathe. Yet there was no whining or complaining when he greeted me, just a warm embrace. And in that glimpse of his life I could not escape some shame as I remembered my *disruption*. I fought tears as I considered Javier's personal story, and wondered onto what makeshift bed he would flop that night.

This column originally appeared in Foster's Daily Democrat, Dover, NH on April 12, 2007.

English and Alex (Part 2)

Several months ago I wrote a column about one of my former students, Alex Chappell, the one who once asked me if I would massage his toes during a break in his soccer game, who didn't know which fork to use when at a formally set table, and who used to eat my apple peels. Thinking back on it, I believe he ate the cores as well. Alex's other eccentricities included some pretty funky hairdos, shorts twelve months of the year, and tee shirts—pretty much *only* tee shirts. He had little patience for traditions, academic slackers, status, or Republicans, and his life epitomized, *if it hasn't been tried yet, it's fair game.* Alex Chappell defined "one of a kind."

It hardly seems possible it was nearly two years ago that Pete, one of our mutual friends, came by to tell me Alex had been killed in a diving accident near Clarkson University to where he had recently returned for his senior year. We spent the next several hours with his Somersworth classmates, teachers, and family—trying to process, trying to understand, trying to cope. Sometime during those hours Patti asked me and a colleague if we would speak at his memorial service. I thought it would be appropriate to share that exact text here as I remember a great former student and an even greater friend.

September 10, 2005
For Steven, Patti, and Steffi

"Chapel"! "Big Mac"! . . . That was how Alex and I most often greeted each other after he graduated. I had an interesting relationship with Alex. He frustrated me by doing as little homework as possible. He made me jealous because he did better in Paula's AP Calculus class than he did in my AP English class. He made me embarrassed that he had more respect for nature than I did. He made me ashamed to go shopping. He had a way of making me feel almost inferior in his presence. You see, Alex couldn't have cared less about brand-name clothes or how he looked. Alex had a deep love for the mountains and nature in general. He was, perhaps, one of the most non-judgmental people I ever knew. You know, compared to Alex I sometimes felt like a right-wing, status-conscious, money-grubbing, drill-in-the-Alaskan-Wildlife-Preserve, tax-cutting, bomb-buying, card-carrying member of the RNC, the NRA, and the Rush Limbaugh fan club.

Really, though, that's only partially true, and even the parts that are true were self-imposed. The fact is I loved Alex, and while he could out compute me with both of his hands tied behind his back and mine on a calculator, I know he looked up to me. I hope and pray that he knew how much I looked up to him. I used to watch him—at times in amazement. For example, he had great friends. I know, because many of them are also my friends. And no one was exempt from his list. Alex's friends ranged from Valedictorians to special-ed students; from athletes to musicians; Christians to atheists; the affluent to welfare recipients. How many college kids do you know who come back home on vacations and play volleyball with a bunch of their old high school teachers? How many guys can you name who go mountain hiking with their moms—and truly love it? How many people do you know who couldn't care less if their clothes come from American Eagle, Walmart, or Good-Will? Who do you know who can solve quadratic equations in their sleep and yet not, as my wife recently reminded me, know which fork is the salad fork at a formal dinner?

There's a passage I frequently cite from a book called *Love*, by Leo Buscaglia, and I nearly always think of Alex when I do. Buscaglia is talking about conformity and he references the trees little children are taught to make in say first-grade art class, the ones with a straight stick trunk and a round top, that look like lollipops—all exactly the same. He goes on to suggest that

Conformity continues right on into the university. We in higher education are as guilty as everyone else. We don't say to people, 'Fly! Think for yourselves.' We give them our old knowledge, and we say to them, 'Now this is what is essential. This is what is important.' I know professors who teach nothing but one best "way," they don't say, 'Here are a lot of tools, now go create your own. Go into abstract thinking. Go into dreaming. Dream a while. Find something new.' Could it not be that among their students there are greater dreamers than themselves? So, it all starts with you. You can only give what you have to give. Don't give up your tree. Hold onto your tree. You are the only you—the only magical combination of forces that will be and ever has been that can create such a tree. You are the best you. You will always be the second best anyone else.

To say Alex was a non-conformist would be sort of like

saying Bill Gates is pretty well-off. My last conversation with him was several weeks ago when he stopped me on a street corner not far from our high school and we chatted while getting soaked in the rain. Alex never listened to any "one best way." He was always looking for "something new" and I know he was a better dreamer than I am. Alex never gave up his tree and he was certainly never the second best anyone else.

Steven and Patti, thank you so much for raising such an incredible son. Thank you especially for sharing him with me.

Two years later, I still miss him, and remember him—each time I approach our soccer field, anytime I set a formal table, whenever I quote Buscaglia, and every time I peel an apple.

This column originally appeared in Foster's Daily Democrat, Dover, NH on August 30, 2007.

Christmas in the Classroom (and beyond)

I'll never forget the Christmas I really scared my principal at St. Mary Academy, Sr. Monica. For perhaps the first, and maybe only, time in SMA history the school, under my direction, was having a predominantly secular Christmas concert. It did include a traditional carol sing with the audience, but the concert itself was titled "Cookin' Up Christmas." I guess by the time the night arrived even I was a bit disappointed that I had not chosen a more religiously grounded program, but the show must go on—and it did.

By the next Christmas I was at Somersworth High teaching English. We don't talk about Jesus too much in public school, even during Christmas, though I do remember my own high school drill instructor, Vinny Ratford, screaming at us regularly during marching band practice that it sounded like we were playing *Oh Come to Jesus* in whole notes instead of *Theme from the Magnificent Seven*. We do, however, during the Christmas season, talk a little bit about the ever fading religious roots of Christmas, a little bit about the childhood magic of Santa Claus, and a lot about the giving, peace, and love which hopefully still symbolize Christmas—and I have been known to read *The Best Christmas Pageant Ever* to my classes.

I remember one Christmas season when the Santa Claus part got taken to heart. My wife MaryAnne and I were late getting home from a church meeting. It was cold and dark, because we'd forgotten to leave the outside light on as usual, and it had snowed. As much as I hate winter I wasn't in the greatest humor as I stepped through the door, stamping my snow covered feet and brushing off my jacket, and probably muttering a few choice phrases about God's sense of seasonal balance in New England! There on the cellar floor, which pointed out that I had again forgotten to lock the door, was a bag with a note sticking out the top. I picked up the bag and pulled out the note, noticing a box of candy canes inside. The note read:

On the twelfth day from Christmas
You are given twelve candy canes.
Because we know how you missed us
These will ease all your pains.

I don't know about easing my pains but they did turn my scowl into a smile as we stomped our way up the stairs into the house.

That was just the beginning. Over the next eleven days the gifts, from as yet an unknown person or persons, most likely student or students, continued to appear, inside the cellar if I forgot to lock the door and just outside it when I remembered. There were eleven icicles to hang in the tree, ten sugar cookies and nine red pens, accompanied by a poem which let me know that it was students behind the gifts:

Nine days bee for Christmas
Hear are nine pens colored read
Becuz yer a teacher
Oar sew you have said?
So when you're students make miss takes
Instead of killing them ded,
Ewe can correct awl those blunders
With you're knew pens that are red.

240

I chuckled as I read it, and my computer spell check is going nuts with red underlines as I type it.

As the days moved on I found a fruit basket, an assortment of gourmet hot chocolate packets with a mug, cranberry bread, bagels, scarves, and more poetry. On the fourth day before Christmas each of the four wrote a poem or letter which came rolled up in a scroll and tied with a ribbon. I ate the food and someday we'll probably wear out the scarves, but feelings put into words last forever. There may have been a misspelled word or two and perhaps an awkward sentence, but I read only love. On the day before Christmas they came to confess and give me their last gift. They presented it *in persons* with the last of their poems:

On the day before Christmas
It is Christmas Eve.
Here is a picture
For our good friend Steve.

This is the last present this year
From your four little elves
To remember us always
And keep on your shelves.

We have really enjoyed
Leaving you presents at night
Sneaking quietly into your house,
Then closing the door tight.

We knew that you knew,
And thanks for not exposing us'
It was obvious yesterday,
But thanks for posing with us.

You've been such a great teacher
We all love your class
So, from our breakfast corner
Thank you and Merry Christmas.

With love,
Kristi
Wysocki
Mari
Mikey

The framed picture of the five of us in the back of my pick-up truck sits on my bedroom dresser but probably needs to get moved to my desk at school. It is a constant reminder of the spirit of Christmas, what great kids I have, and how much love we share.

Thinking about it, I suspect that for many of us Christmas is as much about memories as it is the birth of Jesus, maybe more. Since he wasn't in great health thirty plus years ago, I'm going to guess that Vinny Ratford has passed away. In any event I'm certain he's no longer writing the drills for the Dover High and UNH marching bands, but I never hear the words "Oh Come to Jesus" that I don't think of him! Sr. Monica and I both survived the secular Christmas concert at St. Mary. In fact we both had to admit it was a great success! And you know what? I think Jesus is okay with being remembered through acts of peace, love, and especially giving: a poem, a compliment, a box of candy canes, a mug of raspberries 'n cream cocoa, the Wise Men's frankincense and myrrh, or the Herdmans' canned ham. Merry Christmas!

This column originally appeared in Foster's Daily Democrat, Dover, NH on December 14, 2006.

All About Charlie

Outside of class Charlie talked enough for three people, maybe more. He could have carried his own radio talk show, as host and audience. In class Charlie was an unmotivated, unengaged selective mute. No matter the question it got one of three answers—a blank stare, a shrug, or something that cost him 25¢ for the swear jar. No matter what I was offering—vocabulary, literature, videos, writing—Charlie wasn't buying. At first I thought he suffered from short-boy syndrome, on account of he wasn't very tall. Then I thought he suffered from pretty-boy syndrome, because he was almost too pretty to be a boy. He looked and acted more like a pubescent little kid than a high school student. I would catch him trying to take a fist-full of candy from the "miracle" jar on my desk, though he knew the limit was one a day. He'd just flash his impish grin! I'd make general but pointed comments about "little kids" in high school and he'd grin a bit more sheepishly. But when he'd feed me some line about his homework or a computer crisis, one I couldn't prove was a fib, the grin was pure cunning. Still, I really liked Charlie, and I had this feeling I could win him—if I tried hard enough.

In an effort just to get him to talk I started teasing him, about wearing shorts in the middle of the winter, that belts go around the waist not mid-cheek, about his backpack that was bigger than him, but mostly about his harem, this group of girls that swarmed around him after school—*every day*. I started calling them Charlie's Harem, and each day during our morning check-in I asked him how his harem was doing. It began to elicit a smile. One day I asked him what he had that was so magnetizing. "Charlie, what do they see in you? I mean, no offense, it's not like you're tall, dark, and handsome—you're short, blonde, and . . . pretty." His smiles turned to chuckles.

Slowly, Charlie began to loosen up. He still blew off his writing exercises and routinely failed the vocab quizzes, but he did join the class. Once in a while he even talked. And sometimes he would actually say something that didn't require a quarter deposit. Like I eventually discovered he lived in Rollinsford. "Hey, Charlie, I grew up in Rollinsford!" I found out he lived on a farm where his dad was the manager. "I know that farm. We used to go for bike rides on that road. I even know the lady who owns it . . . No, she doesn't know me, but we used to go fishing and skinny dipping in her pond 'cause you couldn't see it from the road. And there was this big well-like hole in the ground across the street from the pond . . . Yeah, that thing that's got sod-covered brick sides and curves up to a round opening. We'd sneak down there to smoke cigarettes . . . Nope, we never got caught."

Bit by bit I learned more about Charlie and his family. He talked about his farm chores, what he got paid, and how many head of cattle they had. Then one day he said something that really piqued my interest: the previous night he and his dad had birthed a new calf. "Wow! Are you serious? That is so cool; I've never seen anything being born! . . . Really? . . . I'd love to! When do you think it will be? . . . Next weekend? . . . I should be around."

At about 11:00 Saturday morning Charlie called and said the shot they'd given the cow to induce labor should result in about a 12:00 noon birth. I looked at my watch and said, "I can make it."

When I got there the cow was lying in the barn, more like a large shed, really, and a gross one at that. I don't think the cow cared, though, and I know I didn't. I didn't care that I had to dodge cow poop and that I was standing in hay and shredded newspapers soaked with cow pee. I didn't care that slimy looking driblets were oozing out of the cow's . . . *behind*. I didn't even care that Charlie had once again failed Friday's vocab quiz. I cared about watching a living thing being born. I cared about Charlie trying to make the cow comfortable, and about all the things he was trying to explain to me about helping it give birth. All I cared about for that hour or so, as I saw the water break and come gushing out like a small river, followed shortly by the plop of a calf, was what Charlie cared about.

We talked about it all the next Monday morning. I don't remember exactly what we said, but I do remember that that one hour of standing in a birthing shed nearly ankle deep in a slop of urine, hay, cow dung, and afterbirth was a defining moment in my relationship with Charlie. And I remember that sometime while I'd been standing in it I had slipped and said the "sh" word. Charlie flashed one of his grins and promised not to tell—if I put my 25¢ in the swear jar.

I'm not sure if I won Charlie that day or he won me. I do know he read the next book we worked on and he even got a check-plus-plus on one of his vocab quizzes. I also know that he voluntarily rewrote a paper for me five times—until he earned an A! And I know it's not always about me and the classroom, or independent and subordinate clauses or spelling and punctuation, or homework, or grabbing extra miracles. Sometimes it's just about the kid.

This column originally appeared in Foster's Daily Democrat, Dover, NH on November 30, 2006.

Poor Is Perspective

I'm not sure exactly why but rain in the Dominican Republic tends to bring on reflection. Last year the rains drove water under an upstairs door and flowing down the stairway. It also permeated through the second floor patio and dripped from dozens of places into our living room. Much worse than that, it washed away the house of a young friend of ours—literally washed it away into a raging river. That loss was the topic of a column last winter that became one of my classroom "stories" for this year.

Yesterday the rains came again, but only for a day. The San Marcos River, *Rio San Marcos*, swelled but caused no real damage. One of the first things we did when we arrived this year was to have the upstairs patio rebuilt and a new threshold installed under the door. So the worst thing yesterday's rain did was get me a bit annoyed—it also got me to thinking.

The Somersworth School District is regularly referred to as a "poor" district. Heck, we even call ourselves a poor district. We are called a "blue-collar" community. We have a residence-heavy tax base, a large ratio of section-eight housing, and a significant percentage of our citizens living on fixed incomes. We have a harder time each year making the budget, and the tax rate continues to climb. I don't think there is one word of what I've said so far that could even be called an exaggeration.

So where did all my rain-induced reflection intersect with my students and my classroom? Well, yesterday's rain got me thinking about last year's rain which got me thinking about kids which got me thinking about *my* kids (my students) and their education. So I decided to talk with a kid I know and get his take on what going to school means in the Dominican Republic.

Chicho (pronounced chee-chō) is a high school senior. He is a good student, comes from a good family, and lives in a very modest house in an average barrio of Puerto Plata. Basically, to Chicho, school means preparing for his future—and it's serious business. Earlier in the winter he had a chance to go to Chile with his community basketball team to play in a championship series. He would have missed fifteen days of school. When he consulted his administrator the answer was, "not if you want to graduate with the rest of your class." Missing fifteen days of school that close to the graduation, not to mention the Sunday morning "clinics" in preparation for his final examinations, was just too much. I doubt missing an extra-curricular opportunity like that would have gone over very well with most American kids, nor many parents either. But education, and the word of the administrator, is taken very seriously in the Dominican Republic—it is the ticket to a better life.

We talked about life as a senior, his physical classrooms, the school day, courses of study, and the like. School is either held mornings or afternoons. It begins in late August and runs through late June-about the same as our school. His day begins at 2:00 and ends at 6:00, Monday through Friday. His courses include social studies, natural science, chemistry, civics, *educación física* (physical education), art, math, humanities, French, English and Spanish.

Class size and sports are major differences between Somersworth and Chicho's school. We, I think, average about twenty-four students per class, and in Chicho's high school there are about forty students per class. His high school also has neither a library nor a gymnasium. Although they are trying, there are no school sponsored sports—there just isn't money. You can, however, if you look a little bit, often find a lively game of checkers or dominoes not far away. Somersworth of course, like most American high schools, even the poor ones, offers many athletic opportunities throughout the academic year.

There are also, however, many similarities between the two systems. Chicho's school does not offer bacon, egg, and cheese breakfast sandwiches, cereal, bagels, full course hot meals, a sandwich bar, a salad bar, and a snack bar. But there are a couple of small *cafeterías* that sell *jugo y pan* for breakfast and sandwiches or *pastelitos* for lunch. Both systems supply the textbooks students use. Both high schools consist of four years/levels of instruction, and both have some type of dress code, though I personally like the Puerto Platas's much better: a light blue dress shirt and kakis—every student, every day. And like here, bad kids get suspended, typically for two weeks.

I'd never realized what kind of a muse rain can be, what kind of a thought process it can stimulate. I, like most people connected to my school system, always considered ours a poor system. I suspect most of the kids in Chicho's school would consider theirs an even poorer system, but not as poor as many schools in *el campo*, the country town. Yes, Dominican classes are larger and the rooms are smaller, there are no school buses, and there is little if anything in the way of extra-curricular activities. But really, how different are the kids? Most US kids want a car; Chicho wants a motorcycle. Like too many American students, math is his least favorite class. He's nervous about his final exams, and he's scared of going to college. I asked him what he wanted to do in *la Universidad* next year, and he said he plans to become an *ingeniero electro-mecanico*, an electrical engineer. How different are they? Well, as I prepared to leave, I asked my final question:

"What is your favorite thing about school?"

With a sly grin he answered, "*Las chicas.*"

The girls, of course. So what is poor? It's simply a matter of perspective.

This column originally appeared in Foster's Daily Democrat, Dover, NH on May 20, 2008.

I'm a Teacher
Not an Educator

To the hundreds of incredible teachers out there who may read this column: this one's for you!

I spent last Saturday with my grandson. We went to Ron's so I could get my hair cut, and then stopped by school to see if the "Vote No on Article 3" people needed any help getting their booth set up outside the craft fair. I met up with two of my colleagues and several students who were volunteering their time. Around noon we decided to go over to the Good Shepherd School's Fall Foliage Fair in Barrington, where I ran into another colleague along with several friends.

A week ago Saturday I spent the afternoon emceeing the Pumpkin Fest in Somersworth. At one booth or another I saw dozens of my students and former students, and colleagues throughout the day. After he found me, one of my freshmen said, "Hey, Mr. Mac, as soon as I hit the lot I said to Dee, man I don't see him yet, but I know that voice." I played the piano for two students who sang a duet, and held the music for another accompanist so it didn't blow away while the select chorus sang. I ate nachos sold by the senior class, a pulled pork sandwich from the sophomore class, fried dough from the Lion's Club, and the last of the chocolate ice cream from—I don't remember.

Things like that are important. No, it wasn't a Monday, Tuesday, Wednesday, Thursday, or Friday between the hours of 6:00 am and 4:00 pm when I am typically in my classroom, or even 7:25 and 2:35 when I *have* to be in my classroom. It wasn't one of the many after school meetings I have to attend or any one of the dozens of formal workshops I might need to attend. But when teachers are out doing those kinds of things we are setting a visible example. We are actively engaging with our communities. We are supporting the students we teach in ways that extend far beyond the classroom.

Some of my best teaching moments have happened outside of the school day and Somersworth High School, when I was simply setting an example, like freezing my butt off at a hockey game, getting drenched while talking to some of my parents (and grandparents!) at a football game, watching Charlie help one of his cows give birth, speaking at the memorial services for Adam and Alex, stopping to chat with a student who works at Walmart, going to Loudon at 4:00 in the morning to clean restrooms or park cars for a class fundraiser, going to Kevin's concert at UNH, having dinner at Boston's Medieval Manor with the class of 2006, traveling to Derry to see some of my girls in their volleyball championship or to Concord to see John graduate college with honors—after struggling his way through high school. Why are these kinds of things important? Because these are the things teachers do.

I always get a kick out of hearing people in private industry, whose job it is to train employees, compare themselves to teachers. How many times I have heard people say, "Hey, I'm an educator, too. I don't get my summers off and various other week-long vacations throughout the year." Not that there is anything dishonorable with that profession, but I am *not* an "educator." My day does not begin at 7:00 and end at 3:00. It doesn't even begin at 6:00 and end at 4:00. It begins when I leave my house about 5:20 in the morning to greet the folks at Cumby's and get my coffee—and remember I can't push the light at High and West High because somebody might recognize my truck. It ends when I get done with the last phone calls and emails from students or parents at night, usually by the time I go to bed.

Hey, I'm far from perfect. Every once in a while I forget myself and push a yellow light just a bit too far, or do what I call a California stop at a stop sign, and last week at Sunday night volleyball I let a bad word slip. It wasn't an F bomb, it was just a little D bomb, but I wasn't happy with myself.

I wish more people who have influence over kids would realize we teach by example not just by profession, and that we're rarely if ever "off duty." The responsibilities don't end when they graduate, either. I had a former student come in a few weeks ago, a member of the class of 2002, to ask if I'd write a letter of recommendation for graduate school. I was invited to two weddings this summer, class of 1998 and 2002. Did I *have* to do those things? Not according to my teacher contract. According to my contract I did not have to stuff myself with food, play the piano, or raffle off haircuts, oil changes, and gift cards last weekend at Pumpkin Fest, or support the Good Shepherd School and the Vote No on Article 3 volunteers this weekend. Contractually, on Monday morning I *have* to teach *Hamlet* to my seniors and *Romeo and Juliet* to my freshmen. I *don't* have to go to the volleyball game Monday night, but I'm going to, because that's what I, and many of my colleagues, do. We try to set good examples—because we're *teachers* not educators.

This column originally appeared in Foster's Daily Democrat, Dover, NH on October 21, 2008.

Walking and Learning

Forty-six of our seniors and four chaperones just returned from Washington, D.C. I hope you enjoy the trip as much as we did.

Thursday, October 31, 2008
We got away at 7:20 AM, ten minutes earlier than I had planned, and with only two stretch-our-legs stops we were checking into our hotel about 5:00 PM. Forty-five minutes later we were headed for Fuddruckers or Ruby Tuesday's for dinner, after having warned, "No, we are *not* going to Hooters, I don't care how good their wings are!"

By 8:15 PM we had picked and plowed our way through the red line, connected to the blue and orange line and were approaching, with only a few mild complaints about all the walking, the Vietnam Veterans Memorial: the Wall. Our conversation suddenly became soft and sparse. Mike said, "You know, it's one thing to see all these names but when you stop to realize that each one of them represents a life, a person who had friends and family and people who loved them, it's . . . [cough . . . slight turn away . . . silence]." We were a long way from the shelter of Somersworth, and school, and childhood.

Friday, October 31, 2008
Write-it-Down was scheduled for 6:00 this morning—for those who wanted to gather for journaling. My colleague Jackie and I are the only ones here, she in the chair beside me actually writing, me in the next chair by the only plug in the lobby, because the internal battery on my aging laptop has long ago died. Shortly we'll be gathering for breakfast and the first full day

of our much anticipated field trip will begin. We have a tour of Capitol Hill, and the Smithsonian on today's itinerary. I'll let you know how it goes.

Saturday, November 1, 2008
Yesterday was a great day—well almost great. We left for the National Mall on time and got there on time, making our way through the World War II Memorial on our way to the Lincoln Memorial. Of course along the way, as some of my boys tossed a football, I managed to forget, again, that I am fifty-one years old and know almost nothing about sports, except how to watch them. I decided to try and receive a pass—bad idea! After shaking off some pain, I got chatting with a couple of kids as we walked beside the reflecting pool about the awesome history that was represented in everything we were seeing, Abe's memorial growing closer. About 100 yards from its steps I suddenly realized I had forgotten the printout with the confirmation number for our Capitol Building tour. So while the others went on I cut across the mall to Constitution Avenue, flagged a cab, went to the hotel, grabbed the paper, and headed back for Capitol Hill. We did make the tour of the Capitol Building, but I was none too happy I missed Abe Lincoln. Of course I also missed some serious power walking and several potential blisters. A twenty-dollar cab ride and two jammed fingers . . . probably a fair trade. We did lunch at Union Station and then while the kids learned about art and history at the Smithsonian I iced my fingers. Today we're off to the White House and the Holocaust Museum.

Sunday, November 2, 2008
I feel like I should just leave this paragraph blank since I could say little that would do justice to yesterday. After a late breakfast we made our way out to 1600 Pennsylvania Avenue and toured the White House, which was nice and I'm glad I did it, but if I never

did it again it would be okay. Then we experienced what it was we *really* came to Washington for in the first place: the United States Holocaust Memorial Museum. Though I did hear a few more grumbles about walking and blisters, we were able to spend all afternoon there, and it wasn't enough. I've taught the Holocaust in my classroom for years, Elie Wiesel's *Night*, Schindler's List, Wiesenthal's *The Sunflower*, only to discover I've never actually taught the Holocaust at all, at least not in any real and meaningful way. I entered the museum feeling good about having brought my kids on this trip, about being a reasonably learned person, and at least a decent teacher. I left the museum feeling almost ashamed to be a part of a race which could do such incredibly horrible things to other members of that race. I was confronted again, for the tenth or twentieth time—or was it the first time?—with the fact that we all participated in the genocide that was the Holocaust—the Germans by their deliberate actions, the rest of us by our deliberate inactions. The displays of Hitler's rise to power, the reproduction of the train car and the concentration camp bunk, Voices from Auschwitz, the scale model of the gas chamber, and Daniel's story (about a young Jewish boy's survival) all took their toll. The Shoes display might have been the most moving, and the most disturbing—a stark reminder of the lives which once filled them. I remember wondering if my students heard their complaints about their own shoes and feet as they passed the display.

Complaints about Hooter's and sore feet notwithstanding, the short story is it was a great field trip. The longer story is it was so much more. It was tears and laughter, footballs and crematoria, sadness and shame, survivors, saviors, and swollen fingers. It was tired feet and blisters, love and prayer, murder, anguish, and disgust. It was God and no God, Chamberlain and Churchill and Eisenhower. It was stories for our parents and siblings and someday our children . . . all from a fieldtrip learning about a lesson we must *never* allow to be taught again.

This column originally appeared in Foster's Daily Democrat, Dover, NH on November 4, 2008.

What Did You Do This Summer?

In order to respect privacy rights, all names have been changed, including the name of the featured healthcare facility.

Most teachers spend their summers recuperating from the past school year, and trying to store up some energy for the coming one. We might do some workshops, read a new book in our field, go to a seminar, and look at where we want to tweak our course syllabi, things that we hope will add to the classroom experiences and academic growth of our students. And each year we're reminded of summer's brevity.

This summer, though, I did something different, very different, and I can hardly wait to start writing about it in what will be my first assigned journal write this September: *Share with us something from your summer experiences.* While ten months of every year I spend the bulk of my time wrapped up in kids, I just spent the last three weeks surrounded, for the most part, by old people—not just adults, *old* people, and what a three weeks it was!

In early August I started a Licensed Nurse Assistant (LNA) program at Twin Oakes Assisted Living and Rehabilitation Center located in Southern Maine. I attended classes four days a week, and for two of the weeks I had to double up by going to a second facility in central New Hampshire for evening sessions, so I could get all my hundred hours in before school started. On August 20 I took my final exam, and on August 21 I worked my last clinical (floor time). Yes, I'm tired, but I am armed with all kinds of new experiences to bring into my classroom this fall.

Sitting down to lunch, for example, takes on a whole new meaning when you're helping an Alzheimer's resident who can't feed themselves. You and I can skip through the shower in five or ten minutes if we have to. Think about what that means for someone confined to a wheelchair. It might take me four or five minutes to get dressed in the morning, even fewer if I'm in a hurry. But what if I had little to no use of my limbs and someone else had to dress me—in bed—and my only avenue out of bed was to a wheelchair, via a mechanical lift? Time takes on a new perspective, I can tell you that.

For most of the year I help high school students try to become better readers and writers. We work on building and maintaining vocabulary, using greater verbal expression, and remembering to add more details. For the past three weeks I've helped a number of elderly people (and in the rehab wing, some not-so-elderly people) work on building and maintaining muscle tone, using greater range of motion, and remembering how to move their feet or grab a handrail.

Some might find the whole experience heartbreaking. I found it exhilarating. I had conversations with people that to the casual observer were utterly meaningless, filled with unintelligible words, but which added smiles and joy to a number of faces, especially mine. And I can tell you this, I have learned a new appreciation for eating slowly and chewing every mouthful. The fact is I probably enjoyed feeding Martha and Ellen their lunches more than I ever enjoyed feeding myself, and I know I spent more time at it.

At school I spend time reading papers, recording grades, and rewarding academic accomplishments. At Twin Oakes I read charts, record urinary output, and reward physical accomplishments. At school I frequently take time helping students plan the most exciting lives. At Twin Oakes I often spent time listening to residents reflect on their exciting lives. Roger had a rewarding career in the automotive industry; his forte was troubleshooting. Mabel and her family were in the candy business, Audrey was a pastry chef, and I understand apple pie was her specialty. Carl and Joe both served many years in the United States military. How rich their history.

I love how histories cross each other, too. I walked into a room in the rehab unit one morning, after knocking of course, to take the patient's vitals (blood pressure, pulse, temp, and respiration) and heard her say, "Why you look just like Mr. MacKenzie." I said, "Well, that's good, because I am Mr. MacKenzie." She replied, "I'm Mrs. Raymond, and you had my daughter in school." "Yes, I did," I responded, "and the thing I remember most about her is that her smile would light up a room on a sunny day." She said, "It still does!"

At first glance there might appear to be a huge gulf between a high school and an assisted living facility, but there is much more to compare than there is to contrast. About the only real difference is the age of the clientele. I use my knowledge of English in both places as well as my critical thinking skills. I even use my limited math abilities in both places: to compute grade point averages and to compute heart and respiration rates. Yes, at school I feed students information while at Twin Oakes I feed people food. And while in education we periodically change classes and curricula, in healthcare we're more likely to change oxygen bottles and colostomy bags. The reality is that in both places I serve people. And the laughs and smiles of kids? They're little different than the laughs and smiles of the elderly.

I long ago found teaching to be a humbling experience; I have already discovered healthcare is as well. Except for the State Boards, my LNA course is done and another brief summer is almost over—but the fun is about to begin, because school opens and my students arrive in just over a week! I can hardly wait to read about *their* summer experiences.

This column originally appeared in Foster's Daily Democrat, Dover, NH on August 25, 2009.

A Member of
the Audience

I just got forty-five eight to ten page research papers in and the forty-five hours of grading have begun. One of the papers I've already read, Adam's, was on a topic not one of my students has ever researched before: raising the credit requirements for fine or performing arts. Hum, I thought, this should be interesting. He made some good points, not the least of which was the more people are exposed to the arts the more passionate they become about them: music appreciation, drama, performance, etc. These are the kinds of things, according to Adam, that can so positively impact one's life—and the earlier it begins the better, but certainly by high school.

This past Friday night I was able to experience some of that "positive impact" through our own drama department. Usually when I walk through the doors of Somersworth High it's as a teacher. Last night when my wife MaryAnne and I sat down in the cafetorium it was as members of the audience. I didn't have to prepare lesson plans. I didn't have to run any copies, grade any papers, or assess any projects. We were attending the SHS Drama Club's presentation of Somersworth Shorts, a series of short plays, duets, and monologues, and for some two hours I was able to just sit and experience the talent of the dozens of students who were involved in the production.

There was the frog-turned-prince who really just wanted to be his original green, naked, carefree self again. He eventually speculated that if he kissed the girl a second time he might turn back into the frog he missed so much. Finally he decided, "Yuck, I'll just stay a prince!"

There was the ghost of the young man who had taken his life. He was listening to and trying to respond to the lamentations of his bereft girlfriend in My Friend Never Said Goodbye. Seeing these two normally happy and outgoing students portraying such pain over the sudden and, for one of them, unexpected parting, was indeed *sweet sorrow*.

And I got a kick out of The Golden Door, a duet where the immigrant applying for U.S. citizenship knew more about America and being an American, than did the INS agent taking the application. I found myself wondering, in this era of trying to ferret out illegal aliens, just how many American citizens know that the Statue of Liberty does indeed cry out for other countries to "Give me your tired, your poor, your huddled masses yearning to breathe free, the wretched refuse of your teeming shore. Send these, the homeless, tempest-tossed, to me; [boldly proclaiming] I lift my lamp beside the golden door." I think maybe she needs to cry out a bit louder.

I chuckled, too, over The Devil's Defeat, written by one of our science teachers. It was a classic theme, the willingness to sell one's soul to the Devil for money—two boots filled with gold monthly, to be exact. The Devil just couldn't handle it when the bargainer decided inflation necessitated raising the ante and he ripped the souls out of his boots!

The fact is the entire evening was pleasant and unpleasant, funny and sad, light and heavy, frightening and comforting. Little Red Riding Hood went to work as an undercover agent. The Wicked Witch of the West was actually kind of nice, and this really pregnant lady who'd sent her husband for pizza, when he returned empty handed, sent him back out for . . . radishes of all things.

One of the plays I liked the best was written by one of my seniors. It was about a female college girl who fell for a member of a rock band who happened to be attending the same college. At some point each one realized they had known the other from high school, and hated each other. Thankfully they also realized how silly high school squabbles really are and that high school kids do in fact grow up—thank God.

Anyway, that play about former high school students reminded me of my own days at Dover High School when I played Stevie (how appropriate) in the music department's 1972 production of the musical High Button Shoes. The lights, the stage, the glitz, the music, Sarah Shaines playing my mother! It was all drama magic for a fourteen-year-old boy.

Yes, there were a lot of things that made last Friday night special: the lighting technicians who kept the various stage areas properly lit, right on cue, the stage crew who flawlessly and almost seamlessly made the set changes, the prompters who supplied the few forgotten lines, the make-up artists, set designers, and wardrobe specialists, not to mention the eighteen actors and actresses. I saw a student who has gotten into more trouble over the years doing a superb job on that stage. I saw introverts just extroverting all over the place. There were nerds, geeks, brains, airheads, you name it—and they all had one goal: passionately entertaining their audience—and they did it well.

I think we teachers get so caught up in the curriculum of our own academic disciplines we forget that sometimes it's not about labeling the internal organs of a dissected piglet, or correctly solving the quadratic equation by completing the square, or identifying metaphors and similes, or knowing all the relevant factors leading up to the Crimean War. Sometimes it's about playing a green vested prince/frog, or designing a set, or writing a play, or singing and dancing. Or it might be about the student who struggles socially but in front of an audience becomes an entirely different person, or the freshman boy basking in the fact that on stage he's the son of the prettiest girl in the whole school. Maybe we need to be members of the audience more often.

This column originally appeared in Foster's Daily Democrat, Dover, NH on November 18, 2008.

Faculty Meetings and Proms

What could be more unrelated than faculty meetings and proms? Proms are full of youth, and energy, and fun! Faculty meetings are full of age, and experience, and problems, and data, and disagreements, and discussions. Our last faculty meeting, however, was different. Instead of being bored we were interested. Instead of watching the clock we were watching the presenter. By the time it was done, instead of biting our tongues we were drying our tears.

The chair of our Positive Behavior Intervention System's (PBIS) Targeted Team was the featured presenter for this month's meeting and she was highlighting a number of student success stories. Understand that by the time kids get referred to the Targeted Team there are typically some pretty serious issues going on. They may include behavioral problems, failures of two or more courses, suspensions, etc. But at this meeting we were listening to the results of some serious efforts on the parts of at least a dozen of these "targeted" students: office discipline referrals: down; tardies: down; grades: up; failures: virtually eliminated. We listened to the details on some fifteen students who went from being on the verge of dropping out to the verge of graduation, and another dozen who a year ago would have simply quit and gone away; they have all passed the required tests and received their GEDs. We heard about three students who at one time wouldn't say a word in class—they had just returned from being the featured speakers at a state-wide PBIS training seminar. Even these stories, though, did not bring out the tissues.

When the presentation was over somebody said, "Tell the

story about Shelly and the prom." So it got told, and I have permission to retell it here.

From her freshman year, Shelly (not her real name) had been a quiet, shy, and insecure young lady. She rarely spoke unless spoken to, typically kept her head down and her eyes focused on the floor, avoiding as much social interaction as possible. By her junior year Shelly had begun to participate in RENEW, a program designed to assist students who are struggling in school. Within a short time the RENEW leader recommended Shelly join her social skills group where she might learn how to better advocate for herself. Slowly, Shelly began to recognize there was a whole world around her she had tried desperately to ignore.

By junior year Shelly couldn't wait to go to the prom. With the help of family and some friends she readied herself for the big night. It finally arrived and Shelly was beside herself in anticipation. This was a dream come true. She, Shelly, with the downcast demeanor and the low self-esteem, yes, *she* was going to the prom. The only problem was her boyfriend never showed up. Actually that wasn't the *only* problem—her boyfriend went with someone else.

Shelly was hurt but took it in stride, at least on the outside. It just sort of confirmed what she already knew: she was too short; she wasn't pretty enough; she didn't have much money; she wasn't very smart. What could she expect?

But then good things started to happen. Through the social skills group Shelly began to see that she *was* an important person. She didn't have to let other people define her, she could define herself. She began to feel a part of something. Her grades started going up and she began to feel better about herself.

Finally a senior, Shelly really wanted to make her last year of high school something special. She not only worked harder and was more successful in school but she began to take pride in herself. She talked more—in the social skills group, among her peers, even in classes. She stopped watching the floor. She started seeing herself as someone of value. And when spring came she wanted one more shot at her dream of going to the prom, but by the time her social skills mentor got the message it was almost too late.

In a flurry gowns were borrowed and fitted. She found one that only needed minor alterations. But someone overheard what was going on and took her to buy a new gown. Someone else had a friend who was going to hairdresser school and she did Shelly's hair for free. A new pair of shoes came from yet another friend. All was ready, and with a couple of days to spare. The only problem was, Shelly didn't have a date. That is, she didn't have a date until a senior I'll call Gary found out. With the help of some friends at school Gary outfitted himself with a new suit. After hearing the whole story the florist donated the corsage Gary had insisted on buying, along with a boutonnière. Shelly, and Gary, had an absolutely fantastic time, according to Shelly, the best of her life.

She could hardly wait to see her social skills facilitator the next day.

"Gary came on time," she fairly cried! "and he came in to talk with my family!"

"That's wonderful, Shelly," the barely-under-control facilitator replied.

"I told him he didn't have to do that, you know, come in and talk to them. But he said 'Look Shelly, I don't know what kind of boys you date, but this is how it's supposed to be.' And he never left my side all night. He opened doors for me, and pulled out chairs, and I danced every dance, and . . . you know what?" as she finally took a breath, "now I know how I *should* be treated."

That brought out the tissues, and as we dried our eyes and I made my way toward the door I heard Gary saying again, "this is how it's supposed to be," and I thought, ditto, this is how *a faculty meeting* is supposed to be.

This column originally appeared in Foster's Daily Democrat, Dover, NH on May 18, 2009.

www.ingramcontent.com/pod-product-compliance
Lightning Source LLC
LaVergne TN
LVHW011345080426
835511LV00005B/128